STUDYING FILMS

ALSO AVAILABLE IN THIS SERIES

Studying Blade Runner

Sean Redmond

Studying Chungking Express

Sean Redmond

Studying The Devil's Backbone

James Rose

Studying City of God

Stephanie Muir

Studying Disaster Movies

John Sanders

Studying The Matrix

Anna Dawson

Studying Surrealist and Fantasy Cinema

Neil Coombs

FORTHCOMING

Studying Bollywood

Garret Fay

Studying Pan's Labyrinth

Tanya Jones

STUDYING TSOTSI

Judith Gunn

Judith Gunn started her career working for BBC Radio 1 as a chat show researcher. She went on to work for all four BBC radio networks as a researcher, writer, producer and occasional broadcaster. She has worked at the *Radio Times* and has written 6 books to date, including two biographies, a novelisation of a film and *Studying The Usual Suspects* for Auteur. She is now a Senior Lecturer in Media Studies, and an E-Learning pioneer, at Cirencester College.

First published in 2009 by
Auteur, The Old Surgery, 9 Pulford Road, Leighton Buzzard LU7 1AB
www.auteur.co.uk
Copyright © Auteur 2009

Series design: Nikki Hamlett
Cover image © Momentum Pictures
All *Tsotsi* stills are taken from the Region 2 DVD of the film, distributed by Momentum Pictures
Set by AMP Ltd, Dunstable, Bedfordshire
Printed and bound in Poland; produced by Polskabook

British Library Cataloguing-in-Publication Data
A catalogue record for this book is available from the British Library

ISBN 978-1-906733-08-7

Contents

INTRODUCTION

'...I believe the script is totally faithful to the spirit of my book. I would just like to add that in my opinion it is the best screen adaptation yet of one of my works.' Athol Fugard, author of the novel *Tsotsi*, quoted by Miramax in the *Tsotsi Production Notes*[1]

Tsotsi is an African film with more than a hint of Hollywood. Its language is local with a little English and its background is African, but there are no lions and no apparent tribes. *Tsotsi* is the story of an individual African called David, who goes by the nickname of Tsotsi (Presley Chweneyagae). Here is a young man who rediscovers his decency in the face of the problems that challenge so many in modern South Africa and across the world.

Tsotsi contains the unique elements of the African landscape and the familiar maladies of the African stereotype. However, it is also the story of disenfranchised youth and poverty. It features feral children, parentless boys who form themselves into volatile gangs in order to both survive and protect, although often to destroy. It also features the politics specific to South Africa and the universal themes of decency and hope.

It's All in the Name

The name *Tsotsi* means 'thug' and, in a strange irony, it has its roots in cinema representations. In his autobiography *The Long Walk to Freedom*, Nelson Mandela[2] remembers and defines the *tsotsis* as fedora-wearing gangsters imitating the roles of James Cagney and Charles Laughton in the fear-inducing gangster noirs of the 1930s, 1940s and 1950s. It is even thought that the word is a version of 'zootsuit', the name for the wide-shouldered, double-breasted suits of the

American gangster. It may also be related to the words 'ho tsotsa' which means to make sharp, not too distant from our own turn of phrase to 'look sharp'.

Whatever the derivation, the word is not only a name for the individual, but in true representational style it defines the individual and symbolises a generation. The universal theme of gangsters and crime weaves into the specifics, not just of the African continent but of the South African nation and its post-apartheid adjustments as it struggles to reconfigure its nation as multi-cultural, multi-coloured and multi-tribal.

There is a local *mise-en-scéne*, but a universal theme of 'decency'. There is local language, but the universal division between rich and poor, far more pernicious than the divisions between tribes. It is a modern film in a modern township, but it is based on a novel that is nearly 30 years old and set 50 years ago. It stars black South Africans, but the novel is written by a distinguished white South African (Athol Fugard) and the film is directed by Gavin Hood, also a white South African with more than a little Hollywood experience. In addition, Chweneyagae's performance and his life is firmly rooted in the townships and the traditions of a modern urban South Africa.

Representations of Africa and its countries have come a long way from *King Solomon's Mines* (dir. Compton Bennett, Andrew Marton, 1950) and *Daktari* (1966, MGM Television) but it may yet be a while before such representations have the attention of anything but the art house audiences of Europe. Perhaps an examination of this film will go a little way to expedite both the universal and individual themes of this film and its African context.

History

Whilst this is a traditional story, in many ways it does have moments of tension and surprise that will be discussed in this book. It is also a film that is deeply rooted in its context; a context that many students are now unaware of in this country. In chapter two, therefore, there has been some attempt to describe that context and history. It is also worth looking at the little documentary on the *Tsotsi* DVD in the bonus features, *Josias and the Twins*, which traces a day in the life of three children living in contrasting but difficult circumstances in the townships. Some understanding of the life of other teenagers is necessary to the understanding of *Tsotsi*. That said, as Zola (plays Fela) says on the *Making of Tsotsi* documentary 'you can't tell a teenager anything' and *Tsotsi* is also about that.

Best Foreign Language Film – Whose Language?

Tsotsi remains a world cinema offering, indicated by its Oscar for Best Foreign Language Film in 2005. Whilst every country's awards ceremonies may well have a category for best foreign language film, it is inevitable that the one offered by Hollywood is both the most prestigious and the most obvious indicator of the 'other' in film-making. Whether it is protectionism (an attempt to protect the indigenous film industry from having to see all its best awards go to imported films), or whether it is patronising, is debatable.

World cinema has long been a definition of cinema that means films originating from countries other than those that are English speaking. The fact that the film is in a foreign language means that its exhibition will either be subtitled or dubbed into English. It is accepted wisdom that audiences will not read subtitles and find the inevitable clumsiness of lip-synching for dubbing awkward. This, of course, would be truer of English-speaking audiences, who are used to hearing most mainstream films in their own language, than it is of the rest of the world. However, a recent survey by the UK Film Council, has established a change in attitudes.

> **'In the past three years, 33 specialised films have grossed £1 million-plus at the UK box-office compared to 11 in the previous three years, which shows that film culture in the UK is thriving.'** Alex Stolz, senior executive for distribution and exhibition at the UK Film Council[3]

In the 1990s only nine films cleared that figure.[4] The main reason for this, it is suggested, is that the cinema audience is growing in maturity. The main group of regular cinemagoers is still aged between 17 and 35 but there has been a 14 per cent increase in the over-45s visiting the cinema. It has been clearly demonstrated that films that originate outside of Hollywood can achieve success in the mainstream arena, although subtitles remain an issue.

Even with the increased viewing figures, Hollywood continues to purchase ideas and remake them with Western mainstream conventions and language. Japanese films such as *The Ring* (dir. Gore Verbinski, 2003 or *Ringu* dir. Hideo Nakata, 1996) are a clear example of this, as is the frame for frame remake of Spanish film *Rec* (dir. Jaume Balagueró, Paco Plaza, 2007) into *Quarantine* (dir. John Erick Dowdle, 2008), starring Hollywood actress Jennifer Carpenter and including an all-American shooting as an extra.

Mel Gibson filmed *The Passion* (2004) in Aramaic with subtitles and his subsequent film *Apocalypto* (2006) also used subtitles. Ang Lee's film *Crouching Tiger Hidden Dragon* (2003) was exhibited both as a dubbed version and with subtitles - the general critical response was that dubbing spoilt the effect and that the audience would prefer to read subtitles. In some recent television series the use of subtitles has become more common. In *Heroes*, the Japanese characters speak Japanese to each other with the subtitles showing up as integral to the text, appearing almost in comic style. Most recently, *Slumdog Millionaire* (dir. Danny Boyle, 2008) has integrated the use of English and local language apparently seamlessly.

The audience that used to accept subtitles was an audience that used to be more commonly associated with the art house set. While this demographic remains older, it seems that an older group is visiting mainstream exhibition houses. In addition, Bollywood has become an increasing influence in cinema beyond its shores, whilst subtitles continue to be integrated into the text in a manner that is more elemental to the film itself.[5]

Mainstream Defined?

Perhaps one of the main misconceptions that students and audience alike can follow is that art house cinema and world cinema have similar conventions. However, the fact that much world cinema has found exhibition in small cinemas more readily associated with art house styles and conventions does not mean that world cinema does not deal with mainstream themes. In addition, art house films often attempt a clear statement of authorship. The theory of the auteur is evident in many films, sometimes instead of all other considerations, including realism. The auteur is a director whose influence on a film is clear. It may be through the style and delivery of the film, it may be the choice of cast or story, or it may be in the appearance of the director themselves, such as Alfred Hitchcock to John Malkovich.[6]

The narratives of, and delivery of, art house movies might very well attract a smaller audience, as do many films not indigenous to Britain or the US, but this does not mean that a foreign language film is any less preoccupied with a straightforward, mainstream story than the average Hollywood Joe the plumber. These narratives may vary a little in respect of their locations, national preoccupations, such as political systems, or even the way people get on a train or a bus, but they remain mainstream in their style and approach to film story-telling.

In the film world, though, some critics suggest that the reason that foreign language films have become more popular is because they have begun to resemble more closely the conventions the Hollywood narrative. Whilst the language may be unfamiliar to the audience, the style and story are not so different. This, sadly, is not because the audience has become more catholic in its taste, but because the stories offered by foreign language films have become less individual. It may also be that with an increasingly film literate audience, a clear division between the art house movie and the foreign language film as an independent arm of film-making has emerged. There is no reason why the foreign language film cannot choose its genre and adhere to recognisable conventions for a mainstream audience.

Options

A standard convention in the construction of the Hollywood film is to option the idea first -having an idea, script or book optioned by Hollywood studios or directors is known as 'option hell'. A book or an idea can languish for years while studios sit on the idea, neither releasing it nor making it. An option is the process by which film producers, writers or directors pay for the option to make a written work into a film. Options have to be renewed on a regular basis and the author of the piece has to consent. In the case of Tsotsi there had been several attempts to script the novel in the past but none had managed to capture the essence of the story.

One of the problems for a film-maker is that the film is largely the story of an internal journey. There is action and there is violence but it is the story of a boy on the verge of manhood, a young man coming of age and facing moral choices. The novel was first written and set in the 1950s and first published in 1980. By the time of the new millennium there had been several attempts to adapt it and a producer called Peter Fudakowski came across it. He had seen two films scripted and directed by Gavin Hood, a South African actor and film-maker.

Oscar with Gavin Hood, Peter Fudakowski, Henrietta Fudakowski, Lance Gewer

Fudakowski took the risk of commissioning a first draft before he had purchased the rights or the option to film the book. It was a risk worth taking for Hood came back with a good script within two months and together they began the process of refining the script and raising the money to make the film. The final element in the construction of the script was to see what the great man himself thought of it. Fugard had only published one novel, *Tsotsi* - for the rest he writes plays and is well placed to understand the construction of a script. No one need have worried, for the author was pleased with the adaptation and his response to the final product is used by Miramax as part of the publicity for the film.

Tsotsi, then, is a film that, whilst it sought the backing of the Hollywood establishment, and indeed did get some of that backing, it took the risk to bring it to the big screen in a strange language with unknown stars set in a location that carried with it a reputation.

The Language of *Tsotsi*

Tsotsi does have a straightforward narrative, of which more later, but it does also use subtitles even though some of the language is comprehensible to the English-speaking viewer. It was important to Hood to use local talent. He felt, very strongly, that there is a tremendous tradition of drama in the townships. One of South Africa's most established black actors, both nationally and internationally, John Kani, both started and played a starring role in a drama group, presenting many plays written by none other than Fugard.[7] Hood wanted to use that talent and showcase it to a wider audience. However, the new generation of actors use the language of Tsotsi itself - Tsotsi-Taal is the vernacular of the township, a mix of English, Afrikaans and tribal languages. It has its own compelling atmosphere, but if it were to be used in the film subtitles would inevitably follow.

'In bringing Tsotsi to the screen, our primary intention was to make a taut, well-paced, character-driven, psychological thriller. We also wanted to transport our

14

audience into a world of radical contrasts. Skyscrapers and shacks, wealth and poverty, violent anger and gentle compassion - all collide in a film that is, ultimately, a classic story of redemption.'[8] Gavin Hood

It is true to say then that *Tsotsi* conforms to the definition of a foreign language film, but much of its inception and its journey to the screen conform to the more conventional frameworks familiar to a Hollywood audience. Hood cites the idea that it is a 'classic story of redemption', a common convention of many mainstream narratives, not just in Western cinema but in world cinema.

Tsotsi is written by a white novelist in the English language and directed by a man whose work has included appearing as a traditional Hollywood antagonist in the TV series *Stargate SG1* as Anubis.[9] His directorial credits prior to *Tsotsi* were all South African stories but since then he has directed *Rendition* (2007) and *X-Men Origins: Wolverine* (2009).[10] Thus, *Tsotsi* is both a foreign language film and a Hollywood narrative.

The Production

It is standard practice when producing a film from an independent source with little established record and a difficult story to tell to try to use what is known in the trade as a 'piece of talent'. This phrase, in itself, is insulting to the many that have talent yet are not considered well-known enough to sell a film. 'A piece of talent' is not merely applied to the ability of the actor, but to that actor's ability to attract an audience.

Hollywood and the many film-makers who hope to make money out of their projects know the value of *star power*. A star with an admired reputation who can open a film is someone whose presence in the film will mean that the audience will go to see it whatever its genre. This is a privilege mainly reserved for men, actors such as Brad Pitt, George Clooney, Matt Damon, Tom Cruise and the like. Some women are able to open a film, although the accepted wisdom is that Julia Roberts was the first to have that privilege. This ability both confines and extends the industry. Actors such as Clooney use their fame to appear in high-earning films, such as the *Oceans*[11] trilogy, to help finance projects of their own like *Syriana* (dir. Stephen Gaghan, 2005) in which both he and Damon appeared, pursuing a more independent framework of narrative and subject matter.

Tsotsi, however, had none of those advantages and the first decision for Hood as its screenwriter and director was to take a major risk with regard to casting. The investors in Los Angeles were nervous of the idea that the film should be shot using local actors speaking Tsotsi-Taal. This would not only mean the use of subtitles, but it would necessitate the use of an actor in the main role unknown to international audiences. As it turned out Chweneyagae was unknown to all but his local drama group. Hood auditioned some expensive talent in LA to placate the investors and try to compromise by finding recognisable talent that could play the role. In the end, with great regret, he turned down the opportunity to work with some actors who would have made the commercial prospects for the film more certain.

After three weeks he headed back to Johannesburg and began auditioning local actors. Even then the process was not easy. Still fearing the impact of the unknown and the inexperienced, he tried auditioning older actors with some experience, but part of the protagonist's appeal is the hint of childhood about him and the older actors were not sympathetic enough. They came across as hard-nosed gangsters, not teenage thugs who may yet have a chance to change. Hood recalls that he began to doubt his decision to reject internationally recognisable actors.

'I was starting to feel I might have shot my mouth off too soon in rejecting the idea of an internationally recognised actor.' Gavin Hood.[12]

However, as with many successful choices, Chweneyagae's audition clinched the process. He rehearsed a scene with his co-star Terry Pheto (herself a former inhabitant of a squatter town and so genuinely conversant with the language of the townships). So powerful was Chweneyagae's audition performance that he reduced his co-star to tears. He made tangible the reality of the situation they found themselves in - the conflict between wanting to save the baby he had stolen and the fact that such an enterprise was fraught with doom.

The Piece of Talent

It is perhaps, part of the inadequacy of the definition of world cinema that it fails to note that some aspects of certain films do conform to the requirement of containing a piece of talent. The use of Kwaito music, the music of South African artist Zola, who also takes a role as the gangster Fela, brought to the film the 'piece of talent' that, at least in South Africa, would open it.

Zola is the superstar of 'Kwaito'. He is South Africa's most famous musician amongst young people and his music features in most of the film. If the audience listens at the beginning one of the songs is *Tsotsi Yase Zola* and it repeats his name, Zola, in traditional rap style. The title song *Mdlwembe*[13] has a music video that uses clips from the film. *Mdlwembe*, Zola's debut album in 2000, received massive critical acclaim and tracks from his later albums are used in the film. The local audience will, therefore, be very familiar with Zola as Fela, whilst the wider audience is introduced not just to a new actor but a new musician. That is *synergy*, the process whereby two products point at each other; a music video uses clips from the film and points to the film, and the music at the back of the film points to the musician. Synergy is the life-blood of the film industry, tying together phones, cars, musicians and happy meals in a way that benefits all. Zola won Artist of the Year in South Africa in 2002 and had his own TV show on SABC. In this way, the use of a piece of talent with a celebrity status in the country echoes the use of Manuela Velasco in the film *Rec* who also had her own TV show in Spain.

In the last analysis, the film *Tsotsi* was produced and directed by those who had experience and understanding of the Hollywood tradition. It is not a film made by a local director, nor is it strictly speaking a world movie. It combines the long established codes and conventions of Hollywood style with the traditions and history of the new and emerging South Africa. There is, in a sense, a sort of irony as the original tsotsis, or thug, emerged in the 1950s as imitators of the gangsters portrayed in American cinema.

Location

When there was still a possibility that the film would be shot using a well-known Hollywood star, the likelihood was that it would have LA as it chief location. However, the intention of the producers was to make the film as authentic as possible so they shot it in Soweto in South Africa. It is a township that has a reputation for danger but also carries a few misconceptions. For a start its name is not sourced in the African language but is a blending of the words SOuth WEstern TOwnship.

It was set up by the British to house the black populations working in the mines. They were placed in a township away from the main urban centres, populated mainly by rich whites in Johannesburg. Since its population was largely black and of a lower income, it has a reputation for poverty and crime. There is no doubt that large parts of it remain in need of better infrastructure, but it now it boasts shopping malls, suburbs, a four-star hotel and, of course, the original home of Nelson Mandela; now a tourist attraction.

In the end, the authenticity of the film depended both on representing the struggles of a modern Soweto and the changing nature of wealth and enfranchisement in the post-apartheid state. Thus, with cast, location, script and music in place Tsotsi started shooting.

Endnotes

1   www.tsotsi.com.

2   As quoted by Jonathan Kaplan in the introduction to Tsotsi the novel by Athol Fugard, pub. Canongate, 2006.

3   http://www.ukfilmcouncil.org.uk/10300.

4   http://www.independent.co.uk/arts-entertainment/films/features/how-film-fans-fell-in-love-with-subtitles-462402.html.

5   See Man on Fire, (dir. Tony Scott, 1997) or the (TV series Heroes (NBC).

6   Alfred Hitchcock made a little cameo appearance in his films, perhaps as the man missing the bus (North by North West, 1959 (opening titles)) or as the man trying to load a cello onto a train (Strangers on a Train, dir. Alfred Hitchcock, 1951). John Malkovich made a film called Being John Malkovich (dir. Spike Jonze, 2000) in which characters found their way into his head.

7   In 1975, John Kani and Winston Ntosha won a Tony Award for Best Actor on Broadway with Sizwe Banzi is Dead and The Island.

8   Miramax Production Notes Tsotsi.

9   http://www.imdb.com/title/tt0709116/.

10 Source http://uk.imdb.com/name/nm0004303/.

11 Oceans Eleven, dir. Steven Soderbergh, 2003.

12 Final Production Notes Miramax.

13 For an excellent interview with Zola try this link: http://www.guardian.co.uk/film/2006/mar/16/popandrock.

    and for the video this link: http://www.youtube.com/watch?v=uV3nFwUlkYM&feature=channel_page.

CHAPTER ONE – HISTORY AND CONTEXT

The Scramble for Africa

In one of the more sour ironies of European and African history, the justification for what became known as the 'Scramble for Africa' was the attempt by the British and others to stamp out slavery, a trade that they themselves had indulged in since the 16th century. Between 1562 and 1807, European ships took more than 11 million people from the continent of Africa. Even so, as late as 1870 only 10 per cent of the land mass was occupied and held by European countries. What had become known as the 'white man's grave' or 'the dark continent' was still largely the preserve of adventurers, traders and missionaries.

David Livingstone was someone who combined those ideas in his own personal philosophy of Africa. He believed that the only salvation for the African continent lay in the three 'Cs': civilisation, Christianity and commerce. By the 1880s the great and the good of European political life carved up Africa for themselves, without regard for the culture, language or borders of the indigenous populations.

South Africa

In the early 19th century South Africa was known as the Cape Colony and largely fell under the jurisdiction of the British as part of the British Empire. The British had abolished slavery by 1807 and regarded it important that black and white learned to live together under what was known as the 'equalisation policy'.

However, the population of South Africa at that time was partly

Dutch and these settlers were much keener on a separatist policy of settlement whereby they settled and developed according to their culture and religion and the black people lived elsewhere. The idea was that since the populations were so different they could co-exist in their different cultures without interfering with each other.

The Dutch Reformed Church that underpinned the faith of the Dutch interpreted certain biblical evidence as supportive of such separatist ideas.[14] This philosophy, once again, took little account of the fact that the black population in its various tribal divisions already occupied the country. The Voortrekkers, as the Dutch became known, decided (1835–1837) to trek from the southern part of the cape across the Transvaal to the Eastern Cape where they settled.

Their 1,500-mile trek became famous in their history and they established the Orange Free State. However, their relationship with the colonial British power deteriorated and what became known as the Boer Wars dominated South Africa's white history at the turn of the 19th and 20th century.

The wars were hard fought and the discovery of gold in the Eastern Cape turned once struggling farming communities into potentially rich rebels. They rose up against the British who were equally keen to keep their access to the rich lands of the Cape. The British, in fact, were credited with the creation of the first concentration camps there, a forerunner of the 20th century's love affair with war and cruelty.

In May 1910, the Union of South Africa was declared, which allowed for the creation of South Africa under the auspices of the British Empire, and for the self-governing colonies of the Cape and Natal to be the dominions of the Boers. Whilst both British and Boer had suffered desperately in the war, the black South African also suffered severely, not least from the fact that although the Boer Wars were considered to be the wars of white people they were fought on land originally occupied by indigenous black people.

The wars destabilised the traditional tribal communal structure and commenced the urbanisation of the black African peoples, loosening the connection that many had with their original culture. In addition, the structure of the Union allowed for the institutionalisation, and later regulation, of the apartheid system – the philosophy of the separation and subjugation of black and coloured people enshrined in law.

Apartheid

The word 'apartheid' is, in fact, pronounced by most South Africans, as 'apart-hate', exposing its true meaning. I was told this by Archbishop Trevor Huddleston who was instrumental in nurturing and supporting both the Anti-Apartheid movement and its leaders, such as Nelson Mandela, Oliver Tambo and Archbishop Desmond Tutu as well as giving musician Hugh Masekela his first trumpet.

In 1956, Huddleston wrote *'Naught for Your Comfort'*[15], a treatise against apartheid. In June 1959, a significant event in the life of the first incarnation of the novel *Tsotsi*, the South African government attempted slum clearance of the shanties in Soweto. In 1960, more than 50 people were shot and killed by South African security forces when they protested against the Pass Laws that limited their movement into white areas.

The ideology of separatism did not lead to peacefully co-existing societies, but to one community dominating the other. The white farming communities took the land and its resources and built infrastructure that excluded the black South Africans, justifying it with the idea that they did not want or need it. By the 1950s, black South Africans were very aware that they were being excluded and had very little power over their own lives. They could not decide where they lived, what they owned (only in Sofiatown could blacks own their own property), they did not have access to good jobs, to certain parts of the city or the land, or to good water fountains, bus rides or toilets.

Throughout the 1960s, Americans began to succeed in challenging the separatist attitudes that dominated, particularly in the southern states of the US, and the laws of apartheid became more entrenched. Protest movements in the international community were mobilised so that sporting links were cut and trade embargoes and sanctions were imposed both by governments and public response. Cricket and rugby tours were banned, musical links were cut and Mandela and other members of the African National Congress, founded after the Boer war and formed into the ANC in 1923, were imprisoned on Robben Island.

Oscar with Presley Chweneyagae, Nelson Mandela and Terry Pheto

In 1976, a second demonstration, this time in Soweto near Johannesburg, featured school children but, like at

Sharpeville, the South African security forces opened fire on the demonstrators and 332 people died, many of them children. In 1990, Mandela was finally released from prison and was soon to take his place as president of South Africa - majority rule had come at last to South Africa.

Why is this relevant?

While most people would accept that any good film should be able to stand up to examination because of its ability to communicate beyond its localised themes, it is also true that almost every text is a product of the influences that shape its culture. The original *Tsotsi* was written in 1980 and set in the late 1950s at the height of the injustices of apartheid. The film, however, is set in a post-apartheid South Africa, which allows the modern *Tsotsi* the opportunity to represent themes that are common to many young people and black young people around the world.

Endnotes

14   This became known as 'Ham Theology' descendents of Ham separated from the chosen people of Israel. In addition some suggested the story of the Tower of Babel that signifies separation through language was also a support to apartheid. Some of the teachings of St Paul were also used (Acts 12:26 – if you are interested.) Source www.anc.org.za/ancdocs/history/misc/verkuyl.html.

15   Trevor Huddleston, Naught for Your Comfort, pub. Collins 1958.

CHAPTER TWO – NARRATIVE

Universalism

The problem for film-makers and producers is to find a way to appeal to as many people in the audience as possible or, failing that, to make sure that the film has attracted its desired audience. In the UK that means a largely young audience (see chapter five on audience for figures). Once the family, or youth audience, has been removed from the niche market it is challenging to make a film that will be financially successful. The problem for world cinema is that it is already providing for itself a niche market by virtue of the fact that the mainstream market is difficult to interest in the content of narratives from a different world view; this automatically means a smaller market.

One of the ways to offset the possible financial implications of creating a subtitled film that is set in an unfamiliar culture is to ensure that the images and the narrative are immediately recognisable. If the audience is unfamiliar with the language it will, at least, be familiar with the style and characters. The audience will understand the genre and make decisions accordingly. That is the process of *universalism* and producers and directors of films that grow from their own national preoccupations, that become acceptable worldwide, contribute to that process.

This can sometimes attract criticism from the local population. Despite the fact that *Hero* (dir. Zhang Yimou, 2002) was one of very few foreign films to open at number one at the American box-office, its director was slightly defensive about the fact that it was a genre piece.[16] It is an action adventure movie, and that may have seemed like a compromise with Hollywood conventions.

Creative control, audience and cultural specificity have to be balanced by the creator to attract the audience into the cinema. One of the aspects that may tip that balance is connected with who pays for the film. Since the average action movie can cost very nearly $100,000,000, at least, it is likely that mainstream producers and distributors are the only ones who can put up the money. This is not so true, of course, of a film that requires little or no CGI, few or no well-known stars or change of location.

Even so, *Tsotsi* cost $3,000,000 – a lot to get out of one piggy-bank. Even if the company that pays for the film is independent, none can afford to make a film in the full knowledge of making a loss (unless there is some kind of dubious tax advantage). The genre, the style and the narrative of the film must therefore be attractive to an audience so that the text can cover the costs, if not make a profit.

Universality, then, is very important. However much it might be attractive to make a film that is designed to be faithful to its own national space, if it cannot appeal to all but a few of a limited, local audience, it will fail to get distribution as a film or DVD, and its message or entertainment value will be lost. The challenge for directors who source their material from specific areas is to create a film that has international appeal. Thus, issues of genre and the universal narrative become important.

Linear Narrative

A Western element in the narrative of *Tsotsi* is that it is a *linear narrative*; it is a simple story that starts at the beginning and ends with the end of the story. The film uses flashbacks but they are signified simply, so that there is no confusion of narrative structure. In that respect, *Tsotsi* is a Western, or mainstream Hollywood film. Even in the book by Fugard, Tsotsi himself narrates his own life in a linear style.

> 'Tsotsi had always thought about life as a straight line, as undeviating as the one he had taken earlier in the evening in following the beggar from railway terminal, as inflexible as the railway tracks that swept past him, leaving no choice but to be carried where they went.' p.120[17]

The TT Movie

There is a trade description of a certain kind of linear narrative that to spare the blushes of innocent youth I have renamed here. If you do not want to know the original name, skip the next few sentences. In its original form, as told to me by a screenwriter, it was described as the 'arsehole movie'.[18] It takes the form of a race against time (hence my title TT, or *Time Tension* movie). The narrative goes that somewhere in Africa a man is in trouble; he has a cork stuck somewhere embarrassing. The cork is going to explode in 24 hours. There is only one man in the world that can remove that cork and he (of course) is in Los Angeles. The film is the story of how the man, the protagonist, journeys to Africa and removes the cork successfully. It is one of the standard plots and once students can recognise it there are any number of films, TV shows even books that adhere to that principle – the obvious example being the television series *24*.

Northern Stories

A lot of the story telling we are used to in Western culture has its roots in the *Unities of Time, Place and Action*, as posited by Aristotle.[19] He defined a classic narrative as one that combines all these elements to produce a unified narrative, linear in its content. Aristotle, from the warmth of the Fertile Crescent (now known as the Middle East), suggested the style of narrative theory and praxis that established itself in the firesides of the northern hemisphere. 'Once upon a time' is the onset of many a fairy tale in the traditions of European narrative.

The Myth of Fairy Tales

In *The Uses of Enchantment*[20] by Bruno Bettelheim, Bettelheim examines the nature of the European fairy tale. The traditional onset of 'once upon a time' signals to the listener that they are about to enter a different world where not only can a child be eaten but in which the children can defeat the witch. Bettelheim notes the significance of traditional conflicts in society: the figure of the wicked stepmother; the disguised wolf; even the use of the number three (three little pigs, three wishes) hints at a link with the Christian ideas of the Trinity.

Fairy tales like many narratives in the West have a linear content; the very phrase 'once upon a time' signals the beginning, a point in time where the story begins, a journey that the narrative takes as it makes its chronological way through the tale. Traditional Hollywood story telling models itself on the European folktale, owing much of its easily accessible and mainstream narratives to the linear structure.

David Bordwell, Professor of Film Studies at the University of Wisconsin, has spent much of his career discussing and analysing the traditional Hollywood narrative. In *Narration in Film Fiction* (Madison: University of Wisconsin Press,1985) and *Making Meaning: Inference and Rhetoric in the Interpretation of Cinema* (Cambridge: Harvard University Press, 1989), Bordwell tracks the history of Hollywood cinema and analyses how its narratives work both as unified mainstream stories and as interpretations by the viewer. His work on narrative is good for any student who wishes to extend their studies and investigate ideas of the encoding of narrative in more detail.

The Crime Against the Body

While linear stories are accessible and common to the European narrative, their can be augmented by a basic understanding that other cultures sometimes have a different experience of the story. Ideas of time and chronology are not always as important as ideas of morality, fable or ancestry. In some African narratives the understanding of the connection of the physical body to the narrative of life is significant. The body is very important in African mythology – it is the combined memory of the DNA of ancestors. The body is the only thing that colonial powers failed to destroy, and even then 11 million were taken to communities elsewhere in the world as slaves. However, there remains a sense of brotherhood, at least in the reference to each other as 'brothers'. This sense is in the last scene when the father of the baby (John) calls Tsotsi 'brother'; it represents what they share, not what is different.

However, the separation of the body from its source and sustenance is serious and this is Tsotsi's crime - separating the baby from its mother. The significance of the stealing of the baby is not just in the breaking of the line, the line of descendants and the story of the family, but in the breaking of the circle, the damaging of the community. Encased in the linear narrative, written and produced by white South Africans, is a hint of the indigenous black culture's own hegemony, ideas of the importance of the body, of the community of people that dates back, not just to the birth of self-knowledge of the young man himself, but to his connection with his community and his responsibility to it.

> **'Finally it is quite startling to note that the African film-maker, whether unconsciously or consciously as direct descendant of the griot transmitter of tradition, the real 'dominant tendency' which crosses most of the apparent genre, is that of the moralistic fable, descendant of the traditional African tale.'** Ferid Bougedir, p.118[21]

It is no coincidence that perhaps the most widely-known moral fables are those told by the fictional slave of the deep South in America, Uncle Remus. He recounted the stories of *Brer Rabbit*, the most famous of which is *The Tortoise and the Hare*. The stories have attracted some controversy, as their representations of the beguiling and subservient Uncle Remus, along with some representations of black characters as bad, have compounded, not relieved, elements of prejudice and racism. However, Joel Chandler Harris published these stories in the Atlanta Constitution paper in 1879 from the oral tradition he had grown up with in the Southern States, transmitted largely by the Afro American slaves.[22]

Like a fable, Tsotsi is the simple story of a young man's growth into adulthood and redemption, but it does carry the moral fable at its heart. Fundamentally, the narrative invites us all not to steal, for the consequences of what we do may rebound not only on our victim but also on us.

Narrative Theorists

At GCSE, or even AS Level, exam boards do not expect students to be able to quote narrative theorists in detail but, increasingly, the grammar of narrative is important in the study of any media text. Even understanding that film texts, or stories, have a narrative basis and a structure that links to a tradition or influence allows the student to approach the text with a more objective eye. Students are capable of understanding the sequence of a story and keen to offer an opinion on a text, but to gain the skills that allow them to analyse the construct of a text is a start along the route to analysis. Most exam boards nominate the four musketeers of Vladimir Propp, Tzvetan Todorov, Rolande Barthes and Claude Levi-Strauss.

Vladimir Propp (1895-1970)

The study of European narratives has been analysed, not just by Bettelheim, who has much relevance for English literature students, but by Vladimir Propp. He took an analytical approach to fairy tales, much in the way that Bordwell has examined Hollywood narratives. Propp studied Russian folk tales to see what they had in common with each other and to analyse the way in which they were constructed. He sought to identify the genre conventions that established the fairy tale as a narrative identity in itself.

'In this type, the structure or formal organisation of a

folkloristic text is described following the chronological order of the linear sequence of elements in the text as reported from an informant. Thus if a tale consists of elements A to Z, the structure of the tale is delineated in terms of this same sequence.' Introduction[23]

It is Propp that tells the student that there are only eight character roles and he bases his theories on the age-old stories of ordinary folk; villains, heroes and princesses. The characters, he says, that anchor the story, are based on a linear sequence. This sequence can divide into four other elements that define the make-up of the story.

Activity – can Propp be applied to *Tsotsi*? The chart below follows *Tsotsi*'s narrative progress, the characters and some suggested applications.

Propp	*Tsotsi*
the villain	Tsotsi/Butcher
the hero	Tsotsi
the donor (who provides an object with magical properties)	The mother
the helper (partner)	Boston
the princess (obviously)	Miriam
the father (rewards the hero)	The father of the baby
the dispatcher (sends the hero on his way)	Tsotsi's father
the false hero	The police

Activity – Obviously TV cop dramas and Hollywood blockbusters don't necessarily have fairy princesses, heroes and villains, or do they? Start looking.

Propp	Other Movie
the villain	
the hero	
the donor (who provides an object with magic properties)	
the helper (partner)	
the princess (obviously)	
the father (rewards the hero)	
the dispatcher (sends the hero on his way)	
the false hero	

Controlling Ideology

The stories that are told would probably not make sense if the morals and fables that were represented did not relate to the ideology that a community agrees to follow in order to function. Fundamental ideologies are sometimes called 'hegemony' literally referring to the hierarchy of the ideas in a society - such as the agreement that 'crime does not pay' that there is such a thing as human rights, or that all races are equal, everyone should have a vote, couples should stay faithful to each other.

Activity – Identify controlling ideologies in our current community, everything from 'children should be seen and not heard' to dress codes in restaurants.

The ideologies that societies agree to are a part of what allows the community to function in equilibrium: to get up, go to work, come back to a family, drive on an agreed side of the road, agree, even, to go to prison if a crime as been committed. This equilibrium is a standard narrative onset and the majority of narratives take advantage of the uncertainty that pertains when equilibrium is disrupted.

Equilibrium

Equilibrium, then, is perhaps the most dominant wish, if not the most dominant ideology, and serves as an underlying hegemony for the narration of stories it dominates. Almost all stories start with equilibrium and use disruption to set up the task. Examples abound in the conventions of TV drama, certainly most crime drama, and the more formulaic ones, such as *CSI*, are easy to spot.

Activity – Storyboard 6 to 10 shots that move from equilibrium to disruption.

Back story

Michael Mann, the director of *Collateral* (2004), is well-known for his research into character back stories. On the set of *Collateral*, Tom Cruise knew the story of his character from birth to death even though the film is about just one night in his life.

Activity – We know something about Tsotsi's back story, because it is identified through the flashbacks in the film; part of the essential narrative is the way in which Tsotsi rediscovers his back story. We have hints about Boston's back story, which is revealed in more detail in the novel.

1. Boston came from the country

2. He went to school

3. He gained a place at teacher training college

4. His mother worked the fields to pay for his training

5. Boston worked hard and was a good student but he was not good with girls

6. One night he goes out on a date

7. He is clumsy with the girl and she (unjustly) accuses him of rape

8. He is expelled before he takes his exams

9. He cannot go back home

10. He lies to his mother and says he has got a job

11. In fact he has embarked on a life of crime that leads him to Tsotsi

That is Boston's story, but what about Butcher, Die Aap, Fela or any of the other characters? Outline the back story of one or more of these characters in this numbered format.

Enigma

Enigma is merely a posh word for 'puzzle' or 'mystery'. In *Tsotsi*, the idea of a puzzle is probably more appropriate. In the end, an audience has to have a reason to want to carry on watching the story and the 'hows' and the 'whys' are part of that. There is not so much a mystery in *Tsotsi* as there would be in a murder whodunit, but a question as to how he is going to extricate himself from the situation he has placed himself in, and there are some questions about his history, about what and who made him the thug he has become.[24]

Activity

Tsotsi is not a traditional crime story, so its enigmas are more complex, but students could discuss what enigmas there are:

- What is he going to do with the baby?
- How is he going to get him back?
- What will happen when he does? How are the police going to find him?

Zeroes and Ones – binary

A lot of stories work with the idea of opposites when someone is under threat, that there is good and evil. This brings in one of the fundamental aspects of narrative that hooks the audience in, and this is the danger of peril. The baby in *Tsotsi* is in peril and Tsotsi himself is in peril. In addition, the narrative works with ideas of 'have' and 'have not', right and wrong. Whilst films like *Star Wars* (dir. George Lucas, 1977) use ideas of the 'force' and a very obvious binary, *Tsotsi* is more subtle.[25]

Activity – discuss what fundamental binaries are present in the film and how they drive the plot. What or who is Tsotsi's major opposition?

Flashback

Tsotsi has no memories and no real understanding of where he came from. This dilemma is described to the audience through the device of the flashback, snippets of story and memory that describe the character and significant events in his life. The flashbacks show that Tsotsi has been separated from the community both in mind and body and has no concept of his connection with other people or his responsibility towards them.

However, in Tsotsi there is a sense of community, a sense of responsibility towards that community, a responsibility that Tsotsi has to learn to relate to through the salvation of the baby. He does have a sense of the dominant ideology that governs his society, although that might be a combination of influences from the fusion of histories that his community and its ideologies are built on.

In his essay in *Unwinding the African Dream on African Ground*[26], Tafataona Mahoso identifies some elements of the northern narrative that include not just the idea of a linear story, but also cultural linear symbols. He identifies the symbol of Christianity: there is the career ladder and the narrow path to follow. Technology tends to develop, and society tends to progress; northern narratives are eschatological in nature, going from beginning to end. An aspect of this is that other symbolic narratives include ideas of escape from the linear destiny that awaits us all. This escape includes ideas of

39

non-conformity and the outsider, someone who either is, or chooses to be, outside the linear direction of the culture.

In addition, Mahoso states that the mantra of the northern narrative is 'I think therefore I am' the Cartesian declaration.[27] In African thinking such a mantra is much more along the lines of 'I relate, therefore I forge my identity in the community.'

Activity

Other morals in *Tsotsi*:

- Controlling ideology
- Dominant ideology
- Hegemony

These terms are terms applied to the ideas that dominate a society. The idea 'crime does not pay' is a fundamental dominant ideology of most communities. It is one that is clear in *Tsotsi*. What other ideologies are present? Mind map the following ideas.

Innocence

Parenthood

Alcohol

Work

Violence

Redemption and Sacrifice

The redemptive narrative is a common Hollywood convention; even in the simplest of films the audience is made aware of the need for certain characters to redeem themselves for what they have done, either in the back story of the film or early in the narrative. In *Tsotsi*, the redemption is not so neat, for the equilibrium cannot be fully restored. The damage is done, the consequences remain permanent on the life of the mother and of the baby, and on Tsotsi. No one can return to where they were before Tsotsi stole from the family. In fact, what might be considered unfair in the narrative is that it is possible that Tsotsi is the only character who is actually better off, both in terms of self-knowledge and, perhaps, in terms of his long-term, if not his short-term future. The nature of the redemption narrative as a theme is discussed in more detail in the next chapter.

Endnotes

16   http://www.time.com/time/magazine/article/0,9171,400044,00.html.

17   Athol Fugard Tsotsi, Canongate, 2006.

18   Told to a Society of Authors meeting (circa 1993) by screenwriter Robin Chapman.

19   Aristotle, Poetics, Penguin Classics.

20   Bruno Bettelheim, The Uses of Enchantment, Penguin Books, 1991.

21   Symbolic Narratives/African Cinema: Audience, Theory and the Moving Image ed. June Givanni, pub. Bfi Publishing, 2001.

22   Further reading on this indicates that several stories originate from Africa, and that they have their equivalent amongst indigenous communities elsewhere, for reference. http://www.mythfolklore.net/3043mythfolklore/reading/remus/extras/1881_introduction.htm.

23   Excerpts from: Vladímir Propp, Morphology Of The Folk Tale 1928 Translation ©1968, The American Folklore Society and Indiana University.

24   The theory of enigma codes is offered by Roland Barthes.

25   The theory of binary codes is offered by Claude Levi-Strauss, there is a handout at the end of this chapter.

26   Symbolic Narratives/African Cinema: Audience, Theory and the Moving Image ed. June Givanni, pub. Bfi Publishing, 2001.

27   Descartes.

CHAPTER THREE – THE IMAGE OF *TSOTSI*

Perhaps one of the most striking aspects of *Tsotsi* is the vibrancy of the colour – the depth of the reds and browns of the townships, the colour both of the night sky and the daylight, dawn to dusk. The quality of colour lends the film an almost epic atmosphere. Light is used to represent the various elements of the film, both reflecting character and atmosphere. Tsotsi's room is dark; shafts of light shine through the cracks and holes in his walls and often the audience can only see Tsotsi's face half-lit as he hides away. The lack of light hints at the darkness in his being.

It is no accident that the colour is as vibrant as it is for Hood made a conscious decision to film on 35mm film stock[28] as opposed to the usual 16mm, or even shooting the film on digital stock. 16mm does allow for a more gritty feel to a story, but this was done well by Fernando Meirelles in *City of God* (2002), a predecessor film set amongst street kids in Rio de Janeiro with which *Tsotsi* is often compared.

Hood wanted the vibrancy of the township to be reflected in the film, so it was shot in widescreen on a fine film stock. Instead of the verisimilitude of grainy film stock, the film would have a detailed vividness that depicted the background against which the people lived as vividly as the people themselves, as well as perhaps hinting at the complexity and richness of their internal lives.

The idea was to capture every detail of Tsotsi's environment, and thereby lend a sense of intimacy against a wide and epic background. This exposed the detail not just of the colour of the country and the urban African landscape, but of the affluence of the middle class area from which he steals. This is combined with the signification of poverty in the rooms of

Tsotsi and the girl, Miriam, and the grim urban background, which is the living space of the man in the wheelchair.

Colours and Light

The use of 35mm film enhances the colours to a deep richness. There are stereotypical assumptions about Africa that do associate it with colour; the colourful dyes in the clothes; the powerful patterns; the use of the red ochre as a tribal colour; the red earth itself and the deep blue sky. In Tsotsi's town, however, the sky is rarely blue but framed by the dust from the township and much of what takes place is at night.

Tsotsi climbs the steps to his room against a red sky

Nevertheless, there are colour contrasts. The film was shot on location, so the township does have that sense of sand and earth that is associated with Africa. The daylight is bright and he township is framed in Tsotsi's doorway.

Tsotsi talks to Butcher Die Aap with the township in the background

From Tsotsi's point of view, it seems to stretch for infinity. This contrasts very strongly with the darkness of his own small room. The only light that enters comes from a small window or gaps in the wall; there is no doubt that the darkness of Tsotsi's being is represented in the room. In one scene, as he dresses the baby, Tsotsi is at the centre of two crossed shafts of light.

Tsotsi is centred in an X of light as he inspects the baby

Tsotsi's face is often half-lit – particularly when he closes the door on his friends and waits behind it to make sure they leave. They are still unaware of the baby, and in a film noir-style shot, half of Tsotsi's face is lit as he waits for his friends to leave.

Tsotsi waits behind the door of his room

This image signifies, in true noir style, the hidden and divided character of the young criminal. Here is a youth driven to a disenfranchised life of crime and the boy suddenly becomes aware that he has obligations and a choice to do the right thing.

Everything in Tsotsi's room takes place in a private darkness, in silhouette, the kind of darkness that makes Tsotsi feel comfortable, but also the kind of darkness that he suffers, since he has forgotten his name and what led him to his life in the township. Tsotsi's journey is not just one from thug to compassionate human being, but from the darkness of his befuddled memory to, literally, enlightenment.

High-contrast, film noir mid-shot on Tsotsi

Miriam's Room

By contrast, the colours in Miriam's home play with light. She has windows that let in the light. She uses glass to make ornaments that play with light. Her sewing, her clothing and her decoration of her room are all about the use of colour and light, in contrast to Tsotsi.

Miriam's room and her mobiles

What Miriam represents in colour is the life Tsotsi lost with his own mother. With Miriam he becomes David, and that is what he names the baby. At one point in the film he asks her about the mobiles she has made for her baby. One is metal and rusted, and she explains that she was sad when she made it, hence the rust. One is a mobile made of coloured glass. When Tsotsi asks how much she would sell it for he mocks her price, asking 'for broken glass?' She replies that he sees only broken glass but she sees light and he looks and sees that the light falls colour on him. The contrast is simple but clear; Tsotsi inhabits the darkness while Miriam inhabits the light. Unless Tsotsi changes, he is a threat to that light.

Angles

The essential atmosphere of the film, in terms of the angles of shot, is one of intimacy. Hood achieved this by using shot and counter shot - fairly passive shooting but with a great many close-ups. Most people's abiding memory of the film tends to be that of Chweneyagae (Tsotsi), for the film presents him and his thoughts in close-up regularly. When conversations take place they are often in close-up and in cuts between close-ups. When Tsotsi tells Aap that they are no longer part of the same gang (DVD 43:50) for instance, the camera switches between them, with the background of Tsotsi's tiny apartment or the wide expanse of the township behind Aap. When Tsotsi is struggling to leave the baby in the car, the camera switches between the facial expressions of both baby and Tsotsi (DVD 12:38).

However, it is not only conversations between Tsotsi and his antagonists that use the standard cut between close-ups. When Boston, painfully beaten by Tsotsi and recovering slowly with a swollen eye, challenges Fela, the gang boss, to spell 'decency' (DVD 38:55) the confrontation takes place in close-up. The close-ups reflect the intensity of the conflicts that run through the relationships, the internal conflicts as well as those arguments between characters. Their repeated use allows the audience to speculate and anticipate on the strength of feeling in the characters.

In an earlier scene (DVD 7:15) with Boston, Boston antagonises Tsotsi to the point of violence. Each time he becomes more provocative the camera cuts back and zooms slowly in on Tsotsi's growing inner conflict, growing anger, and his growing inability to control himself. The tension ends in the inevitable explosion.

Soap Conventions

The use of the two-shot close-up, often passively represented, is common in soap opera and some have criticised the film for its soap opera conventions. However, this was quite deliberate as Hood felt that it was important to represent the intimacy of the actors by using the passive close-up and allow the actors' faces to inform the story.

> **'As a director, I generally favour camera moves that are motivated by a character's own movement rather than a need to do something cool with the camera. I think excessive camera movement in movies is often motivated by a fear of intimacy with the actors and a concern that the audience will become bored if the camera is too static.'** Gavin Hood[29]

However, the film is not without a variety of shots. Angles are used in the traditional manner; Tsotsi is filmed from a low angle when he is at his most powerful and threatening, and he is filmed almost as a child from a high angle as vulnerability, at the end of the film, is represented.

Activity – Have a look at a three-minute segment from an available soap opera, perhaps a particularly crucial scene, and see how the close-ups work.

- Do you think it is true that director Gavin Hood is using conventional soap camera angles?

- Is this a strength or a weakness?

  Some critics have seen it as a weakness. Do you agree?

The Semiotics of Alienation

Throughout the film, *Tsotsi* is represented as isolated. In the story he is physically isolated from his family and friends. He is also isolated from his memories and, like so many young men of his time in any urban environment, he is isolated from the wealth and opportunity that is both in his face and just out of his reach.

It is a physical truth that the townships are set just outside the wealthy areas of the main city. When they originated they were illegal, they were townships built by the underclass to allow them access to jobs and to family life which working in the mines and the dormitories attached, prevented.

In the modern South Africa the urban township of Soweto now has its own shopping mall and areas of it continue to gentrify, whilst other parts remain isolated from access to the wealth that they have helped to achieve. Like Tsotsi, and the boys documented in the bonus features on the DVD, *Josias and the Twins*, occupants of the townships must cross the environmental boundary of wasteland to enter the middle class suburb that represents all that they cannot have, now owned by a black middle class. This, in itself, may compound the feelings of alienation the occupants of the townships have, as their own community is now divided by wealth and privilege or lack of it.

Boundaries

Tsotsi's isolation is represented by the crossing of boundaries. As he flees from the terror of his childhood he crosses the open wasteland between his parents' home and the pipes of the homeless children that become his shelter. He does so against the background of pathetic fallacy. The thunder crashes around his head, the rain falls and the blue lightning heightens his flight from the cruelty of his father and the memories of his childhood.

When, later, Tsotsi flees from himself and his violence against Boston, he once again crosses the wasteland in the rain and finds himself walking, dead centre, along a tarmac road, back lit in the rain, hood up, in a wealthy suburb. He is every bit the outsider and the weather, and the semiotics of his hood and his silhouette make him a threat. He strikes a universal image of alienated youth.

When Tsotsi finally does steal the car, he raises his hood in the manner that makes the hoody a fearsome image. When he drives it away, complete with its contents, the air is clear and when he abandons the car, the night is clear and the moon is full. Whether or not the semiotics of the moon is used deliberately, it is an irresistible signifier of the mystery of evil.

Regardless, he leaves the car and starts again across the wasteland to the township. Later, when the police discover the looted car in daylight, the high crane shot looks down on them and on the magnitude of their task as they look across the wasteland to the sprawling township below. This is not the Africa where animals roam, but the Africa where modern living struggles with injustice and an inequality that divides South Africa even now, not so much across the colour barrier but the wealth barrier.

Binary

Elsewhere in the film the wide shot is used, particularly in Tsotsi's confrontation with the man in the wheel chair. His pursuit of the old man, who has become paralysed in a mining accident, is pictured against the deserts of the city. In his confrontation with the beggar, Tsotsi is in direct conflict with a form of nemesis. There is a binary effect in the narrative, although Tsotsi's antagonist is not a policeman or a strong man but someone helpless, like a dog, paralysed like his own dog by the blow given to it by his father.

It is semiotics, the similarity between the character's disability and Tsotsi's dog that begins to challenge Tsotsi's image of himself as the thug. However, to begin with Tsotsi is in tsotsi mode; he sees the beggar as prey and the camera angles reflect that.

Even though the city is full of people, Tsotsi manages to find an isolated part that suits his needs. The landscape is derelict and dark, but it is also earthy and every intimate detail of the mini story that is played out against this background is represented in the fineness of the image. At one point the camera offers a wide shot of the boy and the man in the wheelchair. They appear as two small people, in binary, against the giant industrial background that looks as much like any city anywhere, as they play out a crime also conducted in any city anywhere.

In the end, the semiotics of the beggar's condition literally 'melts Tsotsi's heart'. In the book he is described as feeling a growing pain as the memories of the last night in his parents' home come back to him and he sees the dignity in a man who is paralysed like his dog and yet who treasures every day because he can feel the sun on his hands. Tsotsi interrogates the man with a sinister tone, but as he becomes gentler the camera angle favours the man in the wheelchair with the power angle and Tsotsi begins to look more vulnerable. Tsotsi never loses his power but he does lose his threat.

When Tsotsi heads home after the encounter, he leaves behind him the industrial success of Johannesburg and follows the train tracks leading from the city. Once again he is isolated against a backdrop of life going on without him; his only use for the rails is to follow them, not so much ride them.

Truth and Reconciliation

Right towards the end of the film the camera offers a wide two-shot. The bridge between them is the police cars. The two figures are at once reconciled by the possibility of the return of the baby, and alienated by the semiotics of the shot, that mirrors the irreconcilable gulf between them.

Tsotsi and the father try to bridge the gap between them

Semiotics of Redemption

As a representation of his new-found decency he puts on his white shirt, gathers up the baby and takes money to the old man as he passes by. Once at the gate he could leave and run, but he chooses to tell the parents that the baby is there. At this point the ending is very different to the one in the book. The modern retelling deals with the modern South Africa, the concept of a black middle class, and the gate signifies the division between the rich and poor. The gate is an icon of the modern South Africa, quite often it does not work and what Tsotsi does is the nightmare of every middle class South African when it breaks down. Now the gate acts as bars across the divide, prison bars that Tsotsi cannot cross until the gate is opened by the owner who calls him 'brother' in recognition of the history that they share.

At the end of the film, Tsotsi faces the father of the stolen child across the road that divides them. The road does not stretch into the distance beyond them, but is blocked by the gathered police cars and the policemen, but the image still communicates the barrier that Tsotsi has to cross to gain some kind of acceptance in the new society of South Africa. There is one thing that cannot divide them – the colour of their skin.

The use of colour is also simple when it comes to what Tsotsi wears. At the beginning he dons a red top under a black leather jacket. Whilst he does not wear the zoot suit worn by the tsotsis of the 1950s, he has the red and black semiotics of danger and death. When he decides to return the baby, he wears a white shirt. It is a simple but effective signifier that needs little explanation to the media student. It signifies a return to the innocence of the Tsotsi who ran from his violent father, for white is traditionally the colour of sacrifice. In Christian terms, it is the clothing of the one about to be baptised, to enter into a new life.

Finally, as Tsotsi raises his hands in surrender, the camera lowers the angle from behind. Whilst Tsotsi's life may take a turn towards punishment, the semiotics of the gleaming white shirt and the angle of the camera hint at a form of victory, almost a pyrrhic salute. As a final image of the film, it encompasses all that is significant in the colour and makes a striking final moment.

Endnotes

28   Tsotsi Production Notes P10.

29   www. motion.kodak.com/motion/uploadedFiles/tsotsi.pdf.

CHAPTER FOUR – REPRESENTATION: STEREOTYPES

Perhaps one of the most crucial key concepts to understand when studying *Tsotsi* is the idea of representation, in particular how stereotypes are informed by the hegemony of opinion related to Africa and how that is challenged by a film like *Tsotsi*.

Stereotypes are a shorthand description of a character; they are a representation, usually of a human being, whose story can be read immediately. A stereotype is an image of a person or a group of people that contains common *codes* and *conventions* that the audience instantly understands. A writer or producer requires stereotypes in all types of media: in advertising the stereotype immediately defines and appeals to the market at which the advertisement is aimed: a tired housewife trying to get the washing done; a young man trying to be attractive to girls; a cool businessman driving a sleek car.

Generally, stereotypes do not bare particularly close examination. They may be based on the common elements in human attributes, aspects that are easily recognisable, but detailed analysis of a stereotype reveals a cartoon human being. In soap operas, stereotypes are created to signal to the audience the kind of story they are likely to be offered, that of the violent, drunken husband, the buxom slightly older blonde who pulls pints behind the bar, the businessman who will never succeed, for example.

In 30 years of *Eastenders* (BBC), Ian Beale's (Adam Woodyatt) business always hovers between success and, more likely, disaster. Ricky Butcher (Sid Owen) remains intellectually challenged, such that his website entry describes him as not always 'the sharpest tool in the box'. [30] In *Coronation Street* (ITV) Ken Barlow (William Roache)[31] has racked up four marriages and 21 lovers (so far). For an ordinary bloke living in one street he does well, but the audience is used to the stereotype of the ordinary lothario and, once set in it, the audience expects the same scenario.

Back in Albert Square, Phil (Steve McFadden) and Grant Mitchell (Ross Kemp) are brothers who are also thugs, always on the wrong side of the law. In fact, so powerful was the Mitchell brothers' portrayal of the hard men of the East End that Kemp has perpetuated that persona of the 'tough guy' into his documentary series *Ross Kemp on Gangs* (Sky) where Mitchell, the hard man, and Kemp, the actor, combine to investigate some of the most difficult stereotypes in existence. By the same token, the image of Vinnie Jones as a violent offender on the football field, transferred successfully to his representation of a gangster in *Lock Stock and Two Smoking Barrels* (dir. Guy Ritchie, 1998).

Stereotypes and Genre

In the same way as an advertiser might use a stereotype to target their audience, stereotypes can help identify the genre that is associated with that character. Film posters will often identify the stereotype for the audience to make clear the nature of the film. The image on the poster, at the very least, needs to inform the audience of the genre, even if the audience is clear on the cast and the main attraction. Pierce Brosnan, for instance, is an actor associated with action roles, not musicals, but the stereotypical semiotics of the *Mamma Mia!*, (dir. Phyllida Lloyd, 2008) poster: a white background, garlands of bougainvillea, a bride in white, a mother in dungarees, give a clear indication of where the story might be going.

Stereotypes can help define genre but, like all categorisations, they can limit and constrain the story, and thus lead to negative interpretations. It is unwise to assume that all individuals who belong to a certain group also conform to all the common elements of their stereotype. The 'dumb blonde' is one of the most easily recognisable of stereotypes, to such an extent that people will say 'I'm having a blonde moment' if they do something stupid. However, it is unfair to assume that all blondes are dumb. The film *Legally Blonde*, (dir. Robert Luketic, 2001) managed to perpetuate and employ the idea of the dumb blonde, whilst subverting that very stereotype and making the main blonde, played by Reese Witherspoon, both dumb and clever.

Thus, stereotypes are useful to define a genre but also to subvert concepts and challenge preconceived ideas. The expectation of a character can be used to surprise the audience. This is, perhaps, what inspired E Annie Proulx to write *Brokeback Mountain*.[32] She took the traditional stereotype of the cowboy as a rugged outdoor type, able to light a fire, ride a horse, smoke a cigarette in the tradition of one of the great advertising stereotypes Marlboro Man.[33] All that would be associated with being heterosexual; the hyper conservative background alone would be enough to affirm the stereotype as masculine and heterosexual. The stereotype was propounded and advanced throughout the development of the genre in the 1950s through to the 1970s. By the time *Brokeback Mountain* was written, and then made into a film, the stereotype was well established, not least as represented by *Butch Cassidy and the Sundance Kid* (dir. Gregory Roy Hill, 1969) – such that the posters for the two films echo each other.

Stereotypes and Truth

In January 2008, a BA Boeing 747 crash landed at Heathrow airport. The probable cause was loss of power due to ice in the fuel tank. The pilot and co-pilot were quite rightly heralded for their skill and bravery. The next day they made an appearance at BA headquarters where they were greeted as heroes. Their modesty was stereotypically British. They down played what had happened and praised each other's bravery, crediting teamwork and good training and glossing over any suggestion that they might have been in peril. Any outsider observing them would have seen the British stereotype, and applauded it as accurate. Stereotypes can represent an element of truth, and sometimes that element can become an expectation, a prophecy to be fulfilled.

Every insurance company will support, with evidence, the fact that the person most likely to die on the roads is a young man between 18 and 25. Furthermore, he is likely to have been the cause of his accident. However, it is inappropriate to judge every teenager or young male driver on the basis of a few who have accidents or act violently. In much the same way, the capacity of audiences to judge stereotypes is both a tool and a constraint for the film-maker.

Stereotypes and Youth

When I worked for Radio One in the early 1980s, it was my brief to visit various sixth forms and encourage discussions amongst young people about the issues that affected them most and that they would most like to talk about on a show called 'Talkabout'[34]. I would choose four of their number to speak live on the radio and then find and book appropriate celebrity guests. We had to try and vary the topics so that the weekly show did not get repetitive, but every group I visited always wanted to talk about the way they were viewed and treated by older people, particularly the police. The teenage stereotype of the trouble-maker, who drives too fast, drinks too much, shop lifts, makes a noise and starts fights, damages all teenagers by association, and is now at least half a century old. However, anyone visiting many of our town centres will find that young people binge drinking is a problem that both defines the age group and tempts it to then fulfill the expectations of that definition.

Little has changed, it seems. Representations such as *Skins* (E4) and *Hollyoaks* (Channel 4) portray young people as drunk, disorderly and amoral. Representations of British youth such as *Kidulthood* (dir Menhaj Huda, 2006) and *Bullet Boy* (dir. Saul Dibb, 2004) offer issues of colour as relevant, but there are also issues of class, poverty and drug addiction that cross the boundaries of colour and creed. *Kidulthood* itself references the US production of *Boyz n the Hood* (dir. John Singleton, 1991) that followed the story of black young people in South Central LA pursuing different paths, some towards, others away from the life of crime.

Stereotypes and Negativity

Some years ago *The Guardian* ran an advertising campaign entitled '*The Whole Picture*'. The 30-second advert depicted a skinhead running towards a man with a briefcase. The sequence was filmed from three different angles. At first, the skinhead looks as if he is running away from something. The second shot makes him look as if he is about to mug the man, while the final shot makes the viewer realise that his intention is to push the man out of harm's way – the whole picture. (http://www.youtube.com/watch?v=SMKScopMnKI)

Stereotypes and Africa

My first memories of the representation of African countries in the media is that of the civil war in Biafra, a country that lost its battle for independence and became a part of Nigeria. The war was relentless and cruel, and news coverage depicted reports and pictures of black African soldiers dying of their terrible wounds and children caught in the crossfire, suffering the consequences of injury and starvation. Before that, there were the Mau Mau in Kenya and the violence in the Congo. Then came General Amin and the stories of cruelty and strange rituals linked to the tribal superstitions he may, or may not, have had. Add to that the civil wars in Angola, Mozambique, the terrible genocide in Rwanda and the constant story of Zimbabwe as it battles with the consequences of racism and separatism.

In 1984, Michael Buerk brought back reports of a terrible famine in Ethiopia and Bob Geldof embarked upon his crusade that culminated in Band Aid, Live Aid, Comic Relief and decades of fund raising and campaigning. Throughout all this the image of the black African remains stereotyped. Students are familiar with images of the starving child, the mutilated woman, the frightening black African soldier, or the horseman of the Janjaweed in Darfur. Every stereotype is negative and almost all are defined as African as if the African continent were one country, when in fact it consists of independent, self-governing states from the pyramids of Egypt to the penguins of the cape peninsula in the south.

In-between are countries that have never been at war with each other or themselves; there is great prosperity for some and peaceful existence for many more. There is sophisticated urban development as well as starvation, poverty, debt and corruption. There is no doubt that the African continent struggles with huge problems (a brief history of which is found in chapter one). All stereotypes have some root in the truth of what they represent, but to approach individuals associated with their stereotypes, as if they can be defined by that stereotype, is to fail to represent individuals appropriately. It is, perhaps, one of the great strengths of the film *Tsotsi* that it confounds many aspects of the over-simplistic African stereotype.

Stereotypes and Black Youth

One of the most damaging negative stereotypes is, of course, race. In September 1993, a young A Level student by the name of Stephen Lawrence was stabbed to death by a gang of youths in what was thought to be a racially motivated attack. The police investigation was heavily criticised and after a long legal battle, conducted, in part, due to complaints made by Stephen's parents, the Macpherson Report found that the police had been 'institutionally racist'. They had been too affected by ideas of the association of young black people and drug dealing, crime and general violence to conduct their investigation with an open mind. They had assumed some form of guilt on Stephen's part and so had neglected certain aspects of the investigation that would have led them to a successful prosecution of a racially motivated murder.

The essence of a stereotype is that it has some reference to the truth. A stereotype is recognisable because it is a repeated representation. The American police series *The Wire* (HBO) seemed both to confound and to confirm the stereotypes, long perpetuated, of the drug-addicted gangster in the black ghettos of the American inner city, in this case Baltimore. An initial viewing might confirm every negative stereotype in its opinions of youth crime, drugs and black people. *The Wire*[35] is peopled with young men such as D'Angelo, Bodie, Poot and the girl, Snoop, and her partner in crime Chris who serve the chilling Marlo Stanfield. All of them are portrayed as young black criminals, dealing drugs and destroying the competition and each other with merciless and unrelenting violence.

The Wire, however, received tremendous critical acclaim because it delved deeply behind the traditional stereotypes and posited reasons, back stories and understanding as to how the community functioned, both self destructively and as a means of survival. Some of its criminals, such as those portrayed by Idris Elba and Wood Harris, represented ruthless men who were not ignorantly pursuing their business in some random manner, but men who educated themselves, strategised their business and tried to use it to gain access to the higher echelons of Baltimore society. Moreover, not every negative stereotype confined itself to black youth or black adults. Black men and women are represented as functioning successfully in every aspect of Baltimore society, as they do in real life, now to the most powerful role in the US.

Stereotypes and *Tsotsi*

In the opening sequence of *Tsotsi* the audience is presented with a classic stereotype as Tsotsi, flanked by three others, marches down the street. The close-up is on his face, a low angle to signify his power. He is clearly in control. He is not, however, a tribal stereotype. His clothing and his look – jeans, trainers a red sweater and a black leather coat – are those of any urban young man and only the language gives away the location. Onlookers mock him because he is walking rather than driving. He answers their mockery with a universal sign of contempt – a middle finger up to his tormentor.

Tsotsi is every bit the black urban stereotype, an angry young man, a thug by nature and a thug by name, for that is the meaning of Tsotsi. His very name conjures up a South African stereotype that covers the gangs of the shanty towns, young men who run feral in the streets of the townships and who raid the more genteel areas of suburbia. They are often orphaned by accident or illness. Aids is a major cause of their grief, and they form gangs that deal in robbery, drugs and other forms of thuggery. Tsotsi's very name indicates his stereotype. It is how he starts the film, but by the end of the story the viewer finds that, like all stereotypes, there is only a grain of truth in the representation of this thug. He is, of course, an individual brought to his current point in life by a set of circumstances that might make stereotypes of us all.

In addition, Tsotsi is a very familiar stereotype, despite the fact his home is in Soweto and that this is an African story. This is not the story of an African child soldier, nor the story of a starving child, this is the story of a thug whose sophistication and violence could be found in almost any inner city of any country. Tsotsi could be as much at home on the streets of Baltimore in *The Wire* as he is in Soweto. The universal themes of crime and youth poverty are secondary to colour and nationality.

In a recent BBC documentary series, *Law and Disorder*, Louis Theroux rode with the cops on a Philadelphia street and then with youths and gangsters of Johannesburg. In both, issues of alienation, disenfranchisement and drug addiction played out against a very similar urban landscape. The film *City of God* described the lives of young people, neglected and feral in Rio di Janeiro, showing that this is a universal theme with universal recognition across the world.

Moreover, *Tsotsi* the novel was written as a representation of an already established stereotype. The zoot suited thugs that ranged the townships in the 1950s drew their identity and type from American films. *Tsotsi*, in its original incarnation as Fugard's novel, is intended to explore the character stereotype and the story behind the tsotsi type that had found itself a name in 1950's South Africa.

The stereotypes in *Tsotsi* break down further though, so that in the end they are no longer stereotypes but stories of individuals that the film portrays with great understanding and compassion. The principle of *Tsotsi* is to reveal to its audience that no thug or tsotsi is a nameless human being and Tsotsi's name is David.

It is in the characterisation of individuals that what appears to be the stereotypical representation becomes a character. It is also in challenging the assumptions that people have about stereotypes that more is learned about the individuals.

Names

In *Tsotsi*, not only is Tsotsi a name that has a meaning that represents its wearer, but many of the names given to the characters also indicate their character and, to some extent, their stereotype. There is Butcher, Boston, even Soekie and Aap hint at their background.

Tsotsi

When Tsotsi is Tsotsi he is a thug, a gang member, a predator, who seeks out and hunts down his victims. There has been some criticism of the slightly expressionless performance that Chweneyagae gives. His reaction to the violence he commits and the violence he observes is somehow emotionless. Only as he builds a relationship with and for the baby does he begin to see the people around him as individuals. The pivotal scene at the centre of the film is Tsotsi's encounter with the disabled man (called a cripple in the film and the book) played by one of the few established actors in the film, Jerry Mofokeng.

At first Tsotsi sees him, like any other prey, as a man to be hunted down and parted from his money. However, his childlike curiosity overcomes him and he begins to find out what brought Morris to this point, and his cry, just like any other is to proclaim that he is a man. This is a mantra repeated by characters in plays by Fugard (*Siswe Bansi is Dead*). At this point, Tsotsi is offered a choice – he can remain a thug or take a step back towards his humanity and decency.

Butcher

Butcher does exactly what it says on the tin. He is a killer, able to slaughter another human being without a hint of remorse or shame. The fact that life is cheap, and that none of them seem to fear death, is a mark of the society that lives on the edge, close to poverty, war and despair. Butcher knows how to kill a man and does so, in the first instance, with a bicycle spoke aimed at the heart. Of all the characters in the film, Butcher remains in type. What the audience needs to know about him is that he kills quickly and conveniently and would certainly never regret a murder if it made him that much safer. It is important for us to know that, for at the crucial scene in the baby's house, Tsotsi must know that Butcher will kill. Once again, Tsotsi is presented with a choice – to kill a killer or allow an innocent man to die. Butcher, then, is never given the opportunity to redeem his character from the constraints of a stereotyped gangster assassin.

Boston

Quite why Boston has that name is a mystery, but it is given to
him perhaps because of its American connotations, because
it is the name of a foreign place associated with education.
Boston is a failed teacher, someone with an education who
should have known better, and in fact, does know better but
finds himself badly beaten for mentioning it. Boston's downfall
is the same as the downfall for many, both in South Africa and
amongst indigenous populations across the world. Boston is
too fond of alcohol, which causes his failure. But his character
and mind are sound and he cannot but regret his slide into
amoral violence. Boston is a victim, the one who Tsotsi loves
and hates the most.

Aap

Aap grounds the film in its local environment. Aap has a Dutch
name and his articulation seems to be most wedded to the
local Afrikaans and Tstotsi-Taal. Aap is not a leader, he is the
dumb, friendly one who will follow Tsotsi anywhere but who,
on the whole, does not initiate the planned violence. He sees
no escape from his life, but without Tsotsi he must commit to
a less exciting, but solid existence.

Stereotypes and Subversions

The presence of a wealthy black couple in the film perhaps
reminds the audience that countries in Africa have their
rich industrialists and sophisticated aspirations. It is not a
continent of tribesmen, unable or unwilling to function in
the modern world. Neither are all rich black people corrupt;
some are just trying to make their way like any other family. In

addition, the white policeman, Smits, might hint at the history of dissonance between white and black in South Africa. Like any stereotypical detective, Smit (Ian Roberts) does an honest job and seems to have genuine sympathy for Tsotsi, who, as he becomes the individual who returns the baby, steps out of his stereotype as a thug and becomes a young man, a young man with the name David.

Activity

Although stereotyping can be a risky business, from the point of view of equality and diversity, handled correctly it can be an opportunity. Invite the students to mind map a stereotype and share it with the rest of the class. Some things said may need correction but it can progress their understanding of the role of stereotypes in their own minds.

Endnotes

30   http://www.bbc.co.uk/eastenders/characters_cast/characters/character_ricky_b.shtml

31   http://www.corrie.net/profiles/characters/barlow_ken.html.

32   E. Annie Proulx. Brokeback Mountain, pub. Fourth Estate, 1998 Film dir. Ang Lee, 2006.

33   http://adage.com/century/icon01.html.

34   The standard presenter was Andy Peebles, with occasional guest presenters such as John Craven and later, Adrian Love, producers David Winter and Sue Davies.

35   http://www.hbo.com/thewire/.

CHAPTER FIVE – AUDIENCE AND INSTITUTION

Many years ago, when I was a young cub on the Tanzanian plain, I was taken to the local cinema. I can only just remember this, but my parents have confirmed that we saw *The Lion* (dir. Jack Cardiff, 1962). It starred the then 1960's heart throbs Trevor Howard and William Holden and a lion – of sorts. It was based on a novel written by Joseph Kessel, who had spent very little time in Africa. It was the romanticised story of a 10-year-old girl and her relationship with a wild lion that ultimately came to a sad end at the hands of hunters.

The story appealed to me then, and in a way it still does, although its appeal has much less to do with Africa than it does with the idea of being able to control an animal of such power with words such as 'friend' or 'kill'. The scenario was, of course, ridiculous and this was not lost on the audience. Throughout the showing of the film there were guffaws of laughter from the front row (admittedly the lion lacked any sense of presence or reality but we were supposed to suspend our disbelief). When the final curtain fell and the lion lay dead, speared to death by angry African hunters, members of the Masai tribe left the cinema vastly amused rather than offended by the white European representation of their country, their traditions, even their lions.

In the intervening 40 years or so it has sometimes been hard to see how representations of the African continent have improved beyond the Hollywoodised values and representations that only recently have begun to be accepted as part of world cinema. The great Hollywood machine has taken it upon itself to tell the story of the world and its cultures. The barrier of sub-titles and different cultural references have led to an imperialism that overrides other film-makers as if they were incapable of telling their own story, rather than having it told for them.

An abiding issue for the creators and producers of media texts is the reaction of the audience. The fundamental motivation for a producer (though they might deny it) must be money. In order for another text to be made or for the first film to break even the text must appeal to the audience, enough to want to view it and therefore buy it. The creatives (who may include the producers) may have a story to tell, a message to offer, a fantastic art form to bring to the world, but if the audience does not like it then the text fails. In order to avoid failure and to facilitate the success of their script, film or product, the producers and creatives must try to read the audience and fulfil audience expectations.

Definitions

The discussion of audience as a key concept therefore falls into the two areas traditionally defined by educators and they are:

- audience – the discussion of audience in relation to the effects of the text on that audience and it cultural context

- institution – the discussion of audience in relation to the business of attracting and retaining an audience (buyer) for that text

- Hegemony – that is the dominant ideology that both share in the context of their culture and the ideas, politics and history that all share

AUDIENCE

To attempt to get to grips with the mystery of an audience a variety of theories are posited that can be usefully applied to a variety of texts. These are the 'audience effects' theories, although audience effects and responses are probably as individual and varied as the audience itself.

Catharsis

Whilst the uses and gratifications theory is the most commonly offered, the concept of catharsis is easily grasped and introduces ideas of uses and gratifications. Catharsis is the process by which the audience uses the text to indulge in emotions in a guilt-free context. In the film *Good Will Hunting* (dir. Gus van Sant, 1997) the character played by Ben Affleck attempts to chat up a character played by Minnie Driver. She is glamorous, clever and intellectual and he is a builder, not a student at the university. He claims to attend the same classes as Driver and she goes along with it, but a testosterone-filled intellectual jock from the university challenges him. As Affleck flounders in his lie, the audience is filled with sympathy for the character. Even though he is a liar and his motives are suspect, everyone knows how it feels to be embarrassed and out of one's depth. So when Damon's character breaks in and intellectually wipes the floor with the jock, everyone is delighted. The audience indulges in a sense of justice that often does not occur in real life.

In the same way, the Michael Douglas film *Falling Down* (dir. Joel Schumacher, 1993) takes on the frustrations of life, such as traffic jams, shopkeepers who over charge and even gangsters, and beats them all at their own game until his true colours are revealed. Catharsis is a concept that can be demonstrated fairly easily with a simple text and is probably the easiest audience concept to understand. It demonstrates how audiences enjoy (are gratified by) and use the stories they are told to augment their own view of life.

However, the more complex the film, the more likely it is to represent the realities of life and the kind of poetic justice that can constitute catharsis does not occur. *Tsotsi* is a complex text that attempts verisimilitude in its representations and attempts to imitate life. Whilst there are moments of catharsis, on the whole it subverts these expectations in a way that we shall explore later.

Uses and Gratifications

There are, however, other aspects of uses and gratifications that apply. Jay Blumer and Elihu Katz posited the uses and gratifications theory in 1974. It lists a complex set of concepts and emotions by which means the audience is attracted to a text. That list contains 20 uses and gratifications, then divided into four points: personal identity, personal relationships, diversion and surveillance. These categories are largely self-explanatory:

- Personal Identity – the audience identifies with the characters in a text in a variety of ways. They may observe a representation and identify them as similar, or as a role model or a representation to be compared in some way to those they know.

- Personal Relationships – the common use of media texts can affirm real personal relationships. Years ago I worked with a woman who was severely disabled yet became a television presenter for a while[36]. Her parents did not own a television and she often said that she felt more isolated because she could not share in conversations about the latest TV programme than because of her disability.

- Surveillance – the audience is a curious animal and learns in all sorts of ways. Of course, it learns from documentary or current affairs texts, but it will learn from observing the nature of relationships in a soap opera, or from a police series on how to survive.

Uses and gratifications may seem intimidating as a theory, and the individual use of a text by the audience may mean that it is difficult to generalise. One way in which it may become more accessible is by associating it with Maslow's Theory of the Hierarchy of Needs. This theory makes a certain amount of sense of uses and gratifications, as well pointing to some aspects of the film *Tsotsi* that remind the media student that self-actualisation sometimes seems like a very distant aspiration in some parts of the world.

The Hierarchy of Needs

Maslow's pyramid is another key concept that appears to define aspects of common sense.

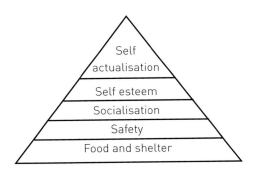

If ideas of uses and gratifications are related to Maslow's pyramid that some of the esoteric aspects seem more appropriate.

- Observing how a text might represent characters such that they belong or do not belong in society appeals to ideas of self-esteem

- The constant appetite that the audience appears to have for crime representations might refer to ideas of survival and safety

- The constant dealing with death might in some ways reassure us and teach us to deal with it, even though it appears to contradict that second tier

- Self-actualisation in reality might be difficult; qualifications, debts, responsibility, ill-health all might conspire against the individual's attempt to self-actualise, but diversion (sometimes known as escapism) might provide the feeling of self-actualisation even if it does not occur. It might even provide the role model and inspiration

Maslow and *Tsotsi*

Perhaps an obvious comment to make with respect to the relationship between Maslow and *Tsotsi* is the social comment. Tsotsi himself is not on anywhere near the fifth tier of the pyramid. His story is that of a youth struggling to stay above tier two. He may have found a small shack in which to live and he may have money to spend on food, but his shack is in an illegal township and the money that buys his food and drink is stolen. In one pivotal scene Tsotsi says to his stolen baby 'You want a home, I'll show you a home, and he takes the baby to the pipes where the feral children shelter. They have no home, no one to look after them, no guarantee of food or safety and they were where Tsotsi came to rest after he ran away from his abusive father. He has, however, grown apart from them, and whilst he sits on the edge of their territory

The children who live in the pipes, once Tsotsi's home

holding the baby the children approach him curiously. They want to know why he's there and in the end one child says: 'He wants to show him his home'.

At that moment, it seems Tsotsi is reassessing his youth and beginning to understand that he has taken a child from a life that will offer access to the privileges of middle class life. Instead, he has placed the child on the bottom tier, a place where even access to food and water is fraught with hazard, and shelter and safety are merely aspirations.

When Maslow's hierarchy is applied to media representations (and there are other models such as business and psychology) it relates to the needs of human beings as they represent themselves to each other. In a media-saturated society such as ours we are dominated by images of glamorous women and are exhorted to build our own houses or redecorate in style. The audience is shown images of happy functioning families in a world of advertised products; society must shop, save, have a pension, a holiday, and it must fear that all this might be stolen by a burglar, serial killer, gang of teenagers or even aliens.

This syndrome has been given the name 'affluenza', an interesting neologism proposed in a book by the same name.[37] Posters at the bus stop, billboards at the station, pop-ups on the internet, sidebar advertising on social networks, pictures in magazines, TV adverts – they all present the audience (or target market) with images of self-actualised people contented by something they have, or the weight they are, or the place they live. And every time we seek to achieve that self-actualisation, the one single fact that we grow old is enough to deny it. No individual can stay young and sleek forever, and so the audience can never self-actualise to the standard the media sets. In addition, if individuals do manage some measure of self-actualisation, the constant stream of media crime representations implies that it can be lost at any moment.

In 2005, research instigated by the Commission on urban Life and Faith, undertaken by the University of Wales, Bangor, and the Children's Society, revealed shocking figures. According to the findings, 70 percent of young people in urban areas have the feeling that life is not worth living, 52 percent often feel depressed and 27 percent have even gone to the extent of seriously considering suicide.[38]

It would be too simplistic to suggest that media saturation of unattainable aspirations and images is to blame for the difficulties young people face today. However, young people do function under continuous pressure to measure up not just to the educational standards imposed on them by the system, but the self-imposed comparisons that individuals make between each other, between what the media represents and what individuals can actually achieve.

Injection and Rejection

Connected with concepts of uses and gratifications is the idea of the hypodermic syringe model. This is an age-old idea of audience effects theory. It is perhaps the most easily understood and the most easily dismissed. The idea is injected into the audience where it is immediately accepted and acted upon. This is basically the use of propaganda and perhaps it is discredited easily because audiences are considered more sophisticated now. They are more able to discriminate, perhaps because they are used to being bombarded with various messages, or perhaps because the audience always has been able to discriminate and was merely underestimated by an elitist analysis.

That said, the evidence in Nazi Germany would suggest that initially audiences were susceptible to the hypodermic syringe factor. Leni Riefenstahl's career was never the same after the 1930s, during which time she published photos for the Third Reich, photos of noble Aryan Germans that perpetuated the propaganda of Hitler's Germany. To some extent it worked and those who believe they think for themselves might want to consider the effectiveness of advertising and to recall the advert that dominates the train station that Tsotsi inhabits; if there was no audience effect there would be little attempt to advertise.

The hypodermic needle theory relates most directly to the definition of the *passive audience* and this is important to get clear, for students often confuse the concepts of passive and active.

Passive audience

The passive audience is, indeed, the audience that settles on the sofa and watches telly, plays the game or watches the film, but then so does the active audience. Thus, what is passive about the passive audience? It is that they accept *passively* the ideas that are sold to them through the media text. They are the victims of the hypodermic needle theory at its most basic. They are most likely to respond to a text by imitating or judging themselves by comparison to it. The famous cases of imitation are examples of passive audiences. In the mid-1990s Benjamin James Darrus and his girlfriend Sarah Edmondson went on a road trip, during which they killed a man and paralysed another. Their inspiration, it was said, was repeated viewings of Oliver Stone's *Natural Born Killers* (1994).[39]

The passive audience however, does not have to be the one that murders a friend because they saw it on TV. They can also be the paranoid parent who will not allow their children to play outside because they fear imminent stranger danger, or they are the many adults who do not go out late at night for fear of crime, or the grumpy shopkeeper who uses technology to bombard young people with an unpleasant sound because a gathering of teenagers is always meant to be troublesome. The passive audience accepts the stereotype and applies it arbitrarily.

Recently, during the run-up to the American election, *The Daily Show*[40] presented by Jon Stewart showed some short clips, with some funny analysis of John McCain and Sarah Palin whipping up the audience into fear of Barack Obama, insinuating that Obama was unknown and therefore to be feared. At the end of the clips, McCain is clearly uncomfortable with the reaction of his audience and is forced to defend the integrity of his opponent, which he does with generosity. However, his audience behaves intellectually in a very passive manner, accepting every bad rumour, every negative connotation and every ignorant comment. They boo when

Obama's name is mentioned; they shout 'traitor', 'terrorist' and 'get Karl Marx out of here'. Stewart likens this to Frankenstein's monster. McCain's campaign rightly focused on his opponent's lack of experience, compared to his own, but the monster he created reacts so passively to the message that they believe everything they half hear about Obama, even to the extent that they believe, because his middle name his Hussein, that he is a Muslim and that that, in itself, effects his integrity.

Active audience

The active audience is easier to explain once it is understood. The active audience measures and mediates what they receive from the text. They too will sit on the sofa and receive the text, but once received they will mediate its message. They know that a representation of violence is not necessarily a call to violence. They understand that representation is about uses and gratifications, not about imitation and unthinking attitudes. Media students are, almost automatically, active audiences. They are inclined to measure and discuss, but nor are they immune to feeling the effects of the texts.

However, there would be no advertising if audiences were completely immune to the constant repetition of images and ideas transmitted through media texts, both moving and printed. In a recent interview[41], Larry Hagman, famous for his portrayal of JR Ewing in the 1970's soap serial *Dallas*, Lorimar Television, 1978, said that he had been accused by a few that his representation of the unacceptable face of the stereotypical Texan made that Texan lovable and paved the way for George Bush. In the same way, some suggest that the representation of black US presidents in films, such as Morgan Freeman in *Deep Impact* (dir. Mimi Leder, 1998) or in series such as

24 (Fox 2001), represented the idea of a black president as a practical possibility, without prejudice.

Audience Positioning

The fundamental premise of the film is that the audience follows a thug and a thief as he steals a baby and attacks his friends, and yet the audience likes him and he is clearly the protagonist of the piece. This is *audience positioning*. It is the way in which the text positions the audience to like who the texts wants the audience to like or dislike. The film *Tsotsi* juxtaposes the audience controlling ideology against the character of Tsotsi with whom the audience has sympathy.

INSTITUTION

The institutional aspects of the industry are the hardest for students to grasp. Their tendency as an audience, whilst not passive in the purest sense, is usually naive. They assume that all films that get made do so because they are good. They assume that popular films become popular purely on the grounds of quality. They do not see the huge amount of marketing and failure that goes into making and selling a film. Perhaps the easiest way to introduce ideas of institution is to define these two concepts:

- Playability
- Marketability

Playability

It is not difficult to define what these two terms imply and the ultimate trick is to combine the two in the one film, but that cannot always be predicted. A film may seem eminently playable and in production it may be well thought of. When it is released it may go down extremely well with the critics, but the audience rejects it and it loses money. Many of these films go on to become highly successful, perhaps as videos and now DVDs, gaining status as cult movies, initially by a minority audience that gradually increases the reputation, and therefore, marketability of a film. Stephen King's *The Shawshank Redemption* (dir. Frank Darabont, 1994) is cited by many as the best film ever, but it did not do great business at the box-office on its initial release.

Marketability

This is the process by which a film is considered to sell well at the box-office. Once again this can be a risky business for films that might be considered to be dead cert successes fail for reasons that cannot always be identified. Kevin Costner sank a great deal of money into films like *Waterworld* (dir. Kevin Reynolds, 1995) and *The Postman* (dir. Kevin Costner, 1997), neither of which did well. At the time, Costner was hot property, a man able to 'open' a film. His very presence in it should have been enough to guarantee its marketability, but the audience is a fickle animal and not always easy to predict. The film business is full of examples of films known as 'sleepers' that are not expected to be particularly marketable, although very playable. The likes of *The Usual Suspects* (dir. Bryan Singer, 1995) have taken the business by storm, while films such as *Titanic* (dir. James Cameron, 1997) are considered by critics to be less than playable but to which audiences still flock.

Target Audience

Whether or not the audience is passive or active it does, to some extent, need to be targeted. A brief look at the Pearl and Dean website's business market data[42] section soon demonstrates that the modern audience is largely under 35, clusters between 15 and 25, and is pretty much even when it comes to gender. The implications of this are that the institutions will target most of their movies at a younger audience. As soon as they classify their movie an 18, they cut out a large proportion of their potential audience. In order to target their audience, various tools are at their disposal, including advertising, synergy (the process whereby two products will point at each other), even awards ceremonies are a form of advertising insofar as the nominations get people talking about the movies.

Activity – divide the students into small groups and get them to 'pitch' a film. They should nominate their genre and support that with suggestions as to cast and director. They should give some description of the plot and of the age group and audience at which they would aim their film.

Sending and Receiving

The problem for institutions attempting to achieve both marketability and playability is related to the way in which they intend the text to be received and the way in which the audience actually receives it. In fact, it goes back to an issue of language. The concept of transmission and reception is an important one in the study of ordinary human communication. Theorists of language[43] posit the idea that the way in which a person communicates has to be both sent and received. The sender will speak with one meaning in mind and the receiver will receive it, hopefully with the same meaning in mind, but as everybody knows the process is not always that simple. When people communicate they often misunderstand each other. They may do so because they are in a state of argument and can be deliberately or otherwise misconstrued.

A conversation such as 'That dress makes you look quite voluptuous' might be interpreted as 'Are you saying I'm fat'. Whatever the level of misunderstanding or understanding, both receiver and sender act and communicate according to their influences. One influence may be the argument that they hear what they hear because of a history of hurt; other much simpler influences may be the use of language - you say 'tomato 'and I say 'tomaito'.

Influence can work both ways. The creator of the communication may censor what they say because they have a preconception about the person they are speaking to – a parent will regulate what they say to a child because they are influenced by their youth. A teenager may censor what they say to a parent in order to hide their activities or because they think their parents will react badly to them. Whatever the style of conversation both, or all parties, will act according to the influence upon them and in the wider context those influences are cultural. They encode what they speak and the listener decodes what is said – intention and interpretation is not always the same.

The problem for the cinema audience in 1963, when I was watching William Holden in *The Lion* in Dodoma, was that the communication of the story was influenced by one set of cultural values (romantic Western ideas about the noble savage, the king of the beasts and a white imperialism that was able to subdue the wild beasts). However, some of the receivers in the audience were influenced by a different set of values related more to their need to survive in the context of nature, red in tooth and claw. The film, which was meant to be a serious story about a child growing up in Africa and experiencing a clash of cultures and a clash with her parents, became a comedy that was at best amusing to those much closer to the reality of Tanzanian wildlife.

Encoding and Decoding

Stuart Hall, who is known as the Marxist theorist of language, sees the system of communication as a negotiation between audience and producer. That negotiation can be quite harsh, for an audience can simply negotiate themselves out of the cinema or away from the text if they don't like it. To facilitate communication, therefore, the producer instigates a process of encoding and decoding.

The producer encodes the text. This will include the use of all the common codes and conventions that the audience is used to seeing employed. There will be camera angles that hint at the power or weakness of the characters, the light will barely reveal them or show them in their full glory, the sound will employ music and effects that hint at the expected interpretation. If the producer gets all that right and the audience interprets it accordingly then the two sides will have negotiated a meaning that they both understand and appreciate. If they fail to do that then the text fails and the audience misunderstands it.

An example of how the encoding and decoding might have different connotations might be demonstrated using the example of the colour of morning. In the film *The Darjeeling Limited* (dir. Wes Anderson, 2007) two funerals are depicted.

The one in America pictures the main characters wearing black whereas in the one portrayed in India everyone wears white. These colours are encoded and decoded differently according to the culture that is their source. In the west and north black is the colour of mourning; in many eastern and southern countries it is white.

The problem for producers is to understand how the influences that shape the way audiences communicate can be reflected effectively. This involves an understanding of the grammar of the host society, such things as the hegemony of our controlling ideology and the universality of some concepts and ideas.

Hegemony

This slightly strange word is another way of talking about the *dominant* or *controlling ideology* that influences, shapes and challenges both society and the individuals within it. It is sometimes defined as the domination of one nation's ideas over another, a definition that is particularly relevant to South Africa and to *Tsotsi*. The cultural history of *Tsotsi* is one full of dominant and conflicted ideologies. The film industry plays one part in transmitting the messages that the audience both here and there participates in both shaping and receiving.

The Hegemony of South Africa: The Scramble for Africa

South Africa is a country where the hegemony, or controlling ideology of its population - for many years its minority population – dominated the thoughts of the society it ruled. In the 19th century many European countries grabbed little bits of Africa. Cecil Rhodes took a part of Southern Africa and named it Rhodesia (now Zimbabwe). Likewise, the Belgians, the Portuguese, the British, the Dutch, the Germans and the French all rushed to get a piece of what they called the Dark Continent. It was known as the 'Scramble for Africa'.

The Dutch pioneers, the Boers, who came to South Africa to build a new life, trekked across the Veldt, fought the British, established their own community and perpetuated the idea that black communities and white communities were best lived separately. That way the white communities could build, mine and develop according to their own commitment to progress, while the black communities could continue to live according to their tribal law. The Boers founded much of their philosophy on a form of Christianity that claimed that God ordained the hegemony of the inferiority of the black races. This was their controlling ideology and facilitated and justified their push to dominate the region, to take land, mine it, build on it and plunder it.

The history of South African cinema is fraught with propaganda both deliberately and ignorantly imposed on the black population in that country. In 1916 a film called *Die Voortrekkers* (dir. Harold M Shaw) was released. It recounted the story of the Boers' war with the British. The black Africans are seen as uncivilised, barely human, and they must be suppressed and then civilised sufficiently to serve the whites.

The filming itself was fraught. The film recounted the Battle of Blood River, the site of a notorious massacre of many Zulu by the Boers. The reconstruction of this battle was also fraught with hostility. White miners who wished to keep the blacks in their place arrived on the set with live rounds and black extras in their turn refused to play dead. In the ensuing filming at least one man died. In retrospect it was lucky that more did not.[44]

However, the depiction of black Africans as little more than foils to be overcome by the self appointed superior Boers did not go away any time soon. In 1938 *They Built a Nation* (dir. Joseph Albrecht) depicted the same Boer battle to establish their nation at the cost to others. It demonstrated in the pre-WW2 era a fondness for the Nazi principles of racial superiority insofar it reflected Hitler's own use of propagandist material to influence and inject a passive audience with national socialist ideas. *They Built a Nation* was none too sympathetic with the British either; its English language version provoked contemporary accusations of propaganda. Only the Afrikaans who already adhered to the ideological retelling of their history adored this version.

The Use of Cinema in South Africa

In the 1930s, one Reverend Ray Phillips attempted to sway black audiences themselves by using film and film narratives to impart to them the ideology of the Western world. This was not the strict and fascist dictates of the Boers, but what seemed to him to be the civilising influences of Hollywood narratives. He exhibited comedies and romances based on monogamous relationships, representing family values and a Disney-led morality and, most popular, Westerns. He called his project the 'moralising project' and developed a sophisticated system of screening films in mining compounds, which served the dual purpose of entertaining the men and inculcating, what he saw, as the correct moral perspective. Whether or not the audience subjected to this screening was truly passive is doubtful – there is no reason to think that a black African is any less or any more prone to audience passivity or to the effect of hypodermic needle theory than, say, the inhabitants of 1930's Germany.

However, the spectators were fond of Charlie Chaplin, who they named 'SiDakwa' 'little drunk man'[45] and Phillips maintained that the showing of a Chaplin film in 1922, when tensions were particularly high, prevented the mineworkers from resorting to violence during a strike. Conversely, the mine companies themselves were concerned, in later showings, that the screening of Westerns might lead the workers to emulate their Western heroes and attempt to overthrow their white occupants and act lawlessly.

Censorship and propaganda, therefore, were the standard techniques for the authorities in South Africa, such that even in 1964 at the screening of *Zulu* (dir, Cy Endfield, 1964) censorship was employed. Only mature, white audiences could see the initial screenings. What is depicted is the slaughter of many black Africans at the hands of the men of Rorke's Drift, who possessed the weaponry to win through. At the time there was fear that the text would enrage black audiences who might be tempted to exact revenge.

For its time the film *Zulu* attempted an accurate representation of the battle of Rorke's Drift and much discussion was held with regard to the costumes of the Zulu women. Interestingly, a dispute arose between the rural women of the tribes and the urban women brought in to increase the numbers. In the tradition of the dance depicted they should have been almost entirely naked, certainly topless, but the urban women, now part of the developing urban landscape, wanted to wear bikini tops, a request considered impossible by the purists. A compromise was reached, both with the dancers, the film-makers and the censors in the Western countries where the film was to become famous.

In fact, filming *Zulu* was to be an exercise in understanding for the young actor, Michael Caine, who was sufficiently aware of the political situation to be uncomfortable with it. One day he observed a black African worker make a mistake. Caine thought the worker deserved a telling off, but did not expect the foreman to punch the man full in the face. Appalled, he began yelling at the man as did Stanley Baker, one of the stars of the film. Baker sacked the foreman on the spot and informed the white gang bosses that such behaviour was not acceptable on set.[46]

However enlightened the actors and writers of *Zulu* may have been, there are still issues with regard to representation.

> '**What is frightening about Hollywood is that it is able to impose its fantasy view of the world upon millions of people. It is impossible to chart the impact of Zulu, an accomplished film upon the mass pysche, but it undeniably perpetuates the mythology of empire, and of white supremacy.**' Peter Davis.[47]

Whilst an active audience might reject blatant messages of supremacy, inferiority or ignorance and the hypodermic needle theory might be less potent than it once was, the constant exposure of the audience to the controlling ideology of white supremacy may have a passive effect on the most active of audiences.

As a footnote to *Zulu*, however, black South Africans were not the only ones to suffer some form of misrepresentation: the relatives of Private Hook, portrayed by James Booth in the film as a drunk and selfish man, sought to sue the film company and redeem their relative's reputation. It was implied by the film-makers that Booth's Victoria Cross was not merited. Hollywood and its narrative can claim many victims. It is littered with narratives that rewrite history from the capture of the Enigma machine (*U-571*, dir. Jonathan Mostow, 2000 – a film in which an American, not a British submarine captures the Enigma machine) to the commercialisation of the story of the Titanic.

It might be easy to criticise the Boers for accepting *They Built a Nation* as a true, rather than propagandist, representation of their struggle but they were viewing the text from their own point of view, their own white supremacist hegemony. Audiences in the Western world view the story of *Zulu* from the point of view of a story of brave soldiers holding out against the odds. The Zulus, meanwhile, including chief Mangosuthu Buthelezi, a powerful figure in South African politics who played one of the Zulus, would rather see the struggle represented, even as losers, than not see it at all.

Cry Freedom

Years later Richard Attenborough was to direct the flight of Donald Woods from South Africa in 1977 in the film *Cry Freedom* (1987). Although this was an attempt to represent the rise of the black consciousness movement and to tell the story of Steve Biko, murdered by South African police, in the end it subordinates the South African element to the story of the white struggle and the *white* sacrifice.

Cry Freedom was very much both an Attenborough epic and a commercial Hollywood venture. It featured Denzel Washington as Biko, already making a name for himself, and Kevin Kline as Donald Woods.[48]

Reviews of the film at the time suggested that it made a strong representation of the white liberal dilemma in South Africa yet the representation of the majority black situation ends pretty much with the end of Biko and the rest of the film focuses on the family's escape. The reading here allows the story of a distant and troubled country to be told in the context of a story not unlike that of *The Sound of Music* (dir. Robert Wise, 1965). The negotiated reading here still allows the ideology of white imperialism, even if that representation describes the problem for black people with more depth than does the film *Zulu*. The white man, in the end, is the one who is needed to progress the objective. Both *Zulu* and *Cry Freedom* are based on true stories, of course, but the good history student will know that with every retelling a different emphasis can be put forward, a different, or slightly different, attitude negotiated and represented according to the ideology that dominates the individual and the culture.

Preferred Reading

Much of what has been described connects to ideas of audiences and what is known as 'preferred reading'. The problem with preferred reading, even for the most active of audiences, is that it is linked to the hegemony of the society that creates the text. If a producer, writer, or director encodes a text in a certain way with certain moral values, for instance the idea that crime does not pay, they will then expect that the audience reads it in that way. However, if the audience is either unfamiliar with what has been encoded or is resistant to it, then the text may either fail to engage with its audience, or be seen as an attempt to impose a view on the audience.

The settlers showed less than no respect for the indigenous inhabitants, their culture, their religion and their borders. The Europeans drew lines and divided ancient tribal lands, they treated the Africans' traditions with contempt and made the black African subservient to their needs and demands. This was the dominant ideology that even the modern South African, black or white, inherited. It was the *preferred reading* of any media text they offered and so powerful was its message that it seemed to convince even the black African population that they were somehow inferior, somehow deserving of the prejudice they endured.

Negotiated Reading

Biko challenged the controlling ideology of modern South Africa. It was Biko, partial subject of the Richard Attenborough film *Cry Freedom*, who formed the idea of the black consciousness movement. He never consented to the hegemony that the black African was an inferior person, but he pointed out that the oppression of black Africans had made them susceptible to the belief that perhaps they were inferior, perhaps that they should allow the white population to lead them, deny them the vote and access to the advantages of an affluent life.

Biko began to negotiate his own reading of the black population's potential, stating that being black was not just a matter of pigmentation but a matter of mental attitude.

In this way, Biko began to change the hegemony of South African culture to the extent that films about Africa, South African and African issues are beginning to have to be encoded in a way that negotiates with the audience a preferred reading that is more acceptable to all the audiences likely to receive the text.

A *negotiated reading* is precisely that – the manner in which an audience mediates the text and responds to it in such a way that the story either develops an independent meaning or the industry itself begins to adapt its representation of the dominant ideology.

Cross Continental Negotiation

More recently, representations of Africa in Hollywood have tried to deal with the conflicts that some readings might consider to be self-inflicted - the terrible genocide in Rwanda for example (*Hotel Rwanda*, dir. Terry George, 2004). Even so, this representation required the Hollywood trappings of named stars to appear in the film and the story itself, although again a representation of historical events, seeks to portray only the culmination of the conflict in the terrible events of 1994 and not really to describe the history of tribal disruption in that country.

The later film *Blood Diamond* (dir. Edward Zwick, 2006) finally gets away from the representation of history, but deals with the darkest secrets of African stereotypes and disruption: the kidnap of children and their employment as child soldiers. This film seeks to link that condition with some sense of first world responsibility. It uses the issue of conflict diamonds, diamonds mined for the rich northern hemisphere countries, without legislation or regulation, whose income is used to buy weapons that facilitate conflicts, kidnap and anarchy.

Each of the above films works with an already established idea, assented to by the Hollywood-influenced culture. The issues move through the ideas of the noble but doomed savage, dominated by the superior technology and strategy of the more 'civilised' culture in *Zulu*, through the representation of the black consciousness movement in *Cry Freedom*, then mutual African conflict in *Hotel Rwanda*, with a final recognition in *Blood Diamond*, that the 'civilised' white north, is no more civilised than its African counterpart. All these films have paved the way for *Tsotsi*, a modern story of Africa, to find its place without clichés against the backdrop of a long and difficult history that still weighs upon its inhabitants.

Empowered?

This is a long way from the use of film by white imperialists on black audiences in South Africa in the 1930s in order to impose on them the ideas of morality, Christianity and political conformity. In just the same way as the history of black people in America is tracked by the lifetime of Barack Obama, from segregation to presidency, the film *Tsotsi* is born of a history of great prejudice and violence based on colour and Western colonial rule.

Activity

How can we apply Uses and Gratifications to *Tsotsi*?

Use and Gratification	*Tsotsi* (use examples)
Personal Identity	
Personal Relationships	
Surveillance	

Activity

Compare the issues of Tsotsi with Maslow's hierarchy to the media-related issues.

- What would Tsotsi really not care about?
- What does he lack and how does he want to get it?
- Has the media affected Tsotsi?

Endnotes

36   Ellen Wilkie had the male form of Duchene's Muscular Dystrophy, despite being female, and was the presenter of a Channel 4 programme on disability called Same Difference – a title she coined. A Pocketful of Dynamite, by Ellen Wilkie, Hodder 1990.

37   John de Graaf, David Wann, Thomas H Naylor, and Vicki Robin, Affluenza: The All Consuming Epidemic, pub. Berrett-Koehler, 2005.

38   http://www.christiantoday.com/article/methodist.spirituality.meetings.planned.amid.shocking.youth.statistics/3829.htm.

39   http://www.trutv.com/library/crime/notorious_murders/celebrity/natural_born_killers/1.html

     Trivia – it turns out that Woody Harrelson, the star of Natural Born Killers, had his own association with murder. His father was an assassin, perhaps for the CIA, certainly served time until his death in 2007. Source http://www.nndb.com/people/666/000023597/

40   http://www.thedailyshow.com/video/index.jhtml?videoId=188473&title=10,000-McCainiacst.

41   BBC Radio Four, Today Saturday 8th November 2008.

42   http//business.pearlanddean.com/marketdata/audience.html.

43   There are various models associated with this idea, but the one described here from the University of Aberystwyth has merit. http://www.aber.ac.uk/media/Documents/short/trans.html.

44   Peter Davis, Darkest Hollywood Zooluology, pub. Ohio University Press, 1996, P.131.

45   Jacqueline Maingard, South African National Cinema, Black Audiences 1920s-1950s, P.69.

46   Michael Caine, What's It All About? pub. Arrow Nooks. 1993, P154.

47   Peter Davis, Darkest Hollywood, pub. Ohio University Press, 1996. P158.

48   Recommended reading Asking for Trouble by Donald Woods, pub. Penguin Books, 1987.

CHAPTER SIX – THEMES

DECENCY

There are no prizes for spotting the main theme in *Tsotsi*
– 'decency' is literally spelled out for the audience by Fela,
who both affirms and defies the traditional stereotype he
represents. Fela is the gang boss, bigger than Tsotsi, the
alpha male, but also aware of Tsotsi and his strength. Fela
is the original zootsuited tsotsi, he is a dapper dresser and a
confident man and that is why Boston assumes that he cannot
spell. He thinks that, like Tsotsi, he is driven to crime by the
circumstances of his life, being orphaned and uneducated, but
Fela is neither.

The audience never knows his history, but whilst he does not
affirm the stereotype of the dumb thug, he affirms the idea of
the clever criminal – a man who may well have a choice but
chooses quick money and a life of crime. Boston is the man
who challenges both Tsotsi and Fela to define decency. The
opening sequence of the film shows Tsotsi's gang picking out
its prey and disposing of him with a bicycle spoke. The film
introduces Tsotsi, Boston, Butcher and Die Aap as ruthless
gangsters who kill without mercy or reason. They are cold
killers who can take a man out in the middle of a busy metro,
but Boston does not like it. He is the conscience of the gang
and is sickened, literally, by the life he now leads.

All the audience knows about Boston, from the film, is that
he has some education. His fellow gang members think he is
a teacher, although towards the end of the film he explains
that he never took the exam. In the film we never know
why, although it is explained in the book. Boston's mother
sacrifices everything to get him educated and he works hard,
aware that this is a great privilege. However, he is not good

with the girls and in his final term a date goes horribly wrong. He is accused of rape, which he states never happened, but he is expelled. He cannot complete his course, he finds odd jobs and finally goes into crime, but to hide from his failure he lies to his mother and sends her money. He also drinks and comes to loathe himself. It is a tragic story of injustice and misery that somehow we understand from the performance that Mothusi Mogano gives.[49]

The film starts with Boston's challenge to Tsotsi about decency, but his provocation only elicits a violent response. Boston taunts Tsotsi and asks if he has ever been moved by anything. Boston lists those things that might cause a man to love, a woman maybe, a parent, a mother, but it is only when he mentions a dog that Tsotsi responds and beats him, almost literally, to a pulp. This moment, this challenge to decency sets Tsotsi on the path that leads him, in the end, to some form of decency. The terrible beating ends before he has killed Boston and he runs into the night, out into the storm across the scrub to another world, which he also tries to damage. Tsotsi steals a car, and in it is a baby.

It is not a new idea that the innocence of a baby leads a hardened man to love and humanity, but it is a simple device that acts almost like Hitchcock's MacGuffin.[50] The baby makes a limited appearance in the film since Tsotsi barely knows what to do with the child, and for the most part it is kept under the bed or hidden in a bag. However, one look from the baby, one small cry and even Tsotsi cannot deny his instinct to look after the defenceless child. Once he has awoken that sense of decency there is no going back.

The theme is developed via the device of looking after the baby, trying to find him milk, trying to change him, trying to get him to keep quiet or go to sleep. Tsotsi has a limited sense of responsibility and it is touch and go whether the baby will survive, but once he has taken the baby from the car he knows he must try to look after it. It is a small matter of basic child psychology - to give the irresponsible one something to look after and he or she will soon find a sense of maturity. The first hint that the audience gets that Tsotsi is beginning to change is when he does not rob and kill the disabled beggar, who calls himself a cripple (see Textual Analysis activity at the end of the chapter).

Decency and Food

The problem with a sense of decency is that it then presents the protagonist with a dilemma. In Tsotsi's case this ranges between his desire to keep the baby and look after it and how to avoid discovery of his crime. Initially, it is hard to tell whether Tsotsi feels his dilemma more greatly because he fears getting caught more than wanting to keep the baby. Once again in the book there is a greater back story to Tsotsi that sheds some light on the efforts he goes to look after the baby. In the film Tsotsi already has condensed milk in his room. This is not unusual in places where heat is plentiful and fridges are rare.

However, in the book Tsotsi does not have any condensed milk and must buy it. The description of Tsotsi (spotted by the storekeeper as 'the type'[51]) waiting and watching for hours before he decides to go into the shop portrays him as a man or boy to be feared. His presence unnerves the storekeeper and this is augmented by descriptions of Tsotsi walking down the street. Fela reflects this in the opening sequence in the film but that sequence is qualified by mockery about his inability to drive, which becomes significant to the plot. In the book, when Tsotsi walks down the street, mothers bring their children in to shelter them from him 'big brave men stepped aside to let him pass'[52].

While the camera centres on Tsotsi at the beginning at a slightly low angle and flanked by his gang, there is not quite the impact of fear that the book portrays. In the book, Tsotsi is more like the character of Omar, represented in the American crime series *The Wire*, set in urban Baltimore. When Omar walks down the street people cry 'Omar comin' and hide their children and bolt their doors against him. Though separated by culture and geography, Tsotsi and Omar are one and the same. To get an indication of the power of Tsotsi's image and the apparently irredeemable elements of his character it might be worth taking a look at episodes of *The Wire* that feature Omar.[53]

Tsotsi then has a long way to go to decency, but this is a simple film about a complex character and it can never quite escape its context. Since the end of apartheid, South Africans, both black and white, have attempted to heal the rifts that have divided them by entering upon a process of truth and reconciliation. Former enemies seek amnesty before the Truth and Reconciliation Commission, whereby perpetrators of former crimes such as torture, betrayal, or worse, confess to their victims and attempts are made at reconciliation. Tsotsi may be a criminal but one in a country that can accept complexities of someone who can both behave badly and, in some ways become redeemed.

Aside from being discovered, Tsotsi's main dilemma is to feed the baby but the condensed milk does not go well. Ants find the condensed milk and the baby. They are, for the purposes of the film, CGI ants and an example of how CGI can augment the verisimilitude of a text in the most realistic of representations. However, students in England may not recognise the danger of ants in Africa – most ants are equipped with acid or bite but in Africa soldier ants can be deadly. They do not traverse but continue in a straight line in massive numbers. In my own childhood in Tanzania our home help, who had his home and a little land at the bottom of our garden, came running in one night because the soldier ants had got into the shamba (hut) and were marching over the children's beds. We housed him for the night and in the morning the ants had marched through. This scene in *Tsotsi* is a serious representation of the danger that all face in the townships. Tsotsi must find food for the baby; he knows enough to know it cries because it is hungry and that condensed milk is not good for it.

Part of Tsotsi's move towards decency is not just his relationship with the baby or the reproaches offered by Boston, but his relationship with Miriam.

Miriam

Miriam is a decent woman and she was married to a decent man. She is the binary opposite of Tsotsi, not just in terms of her gender, her motherhood or even the colours in her room, but because she is decent, despite the context, despite the poverty and the loss she has suffered. Probably to someone like Tsotsi she remains a decent human being, beginning to carve out a decent life. When the audience first meets her she is filling up the teapot of an old man who likes an afternoon cup of tea. In the book she allows him to go ahead of her in the water queue and fills his pot for him whereas in the film the audience is introduced to her at the end of this process. The audience is given enough to understand that she is a good woman and the unpleasant mockery that she suffers from Butcher and Die Aap emphasises both that and her vulnerability.

The scene where Tsotsi breaks in after her was the audition scene for Chweneyagae. It was his representation of this both tender and violent scene that won him the part. The tension in the scene at first viewing is heightened. The audience knows that Tsotsi is a killer and a thug and he could just as easily kill Miriam and her baby. Hollywood conventions dictate that this scene, where the handsome young couple seem to get off on the wrong foot, will demand that by the end of the film they are in love. *Tsotsi*, as a film, makes some concessions to this convention, but it is subtle and offers only the merest hint of such a resolution. Miriam's main purpose is to feed the baby and to stir in Tsotsi memories of his mother and of his name, David. It is the tenderness of the mother that reminds him of his own mother and his dog, so badly damaged by a drunken father.

By the end of the film Tsotsi has become aware of the value of a mother's love. It is this recognition of its value, precisely because he lost it, that means that he finds the decency that Boston demands of him. In some mild way he enters upon his own 12-step programme[54]. He decides that he must nurse and apologise to Boston. He agrees also to take the child back to its wounded mother and he even turns down Miriam's offer to take it back for him, an act that even a week before he would probably have allowed.

Sacrifice

In the meantime, Tsotsi must learn that good parents are often driven to commit terrible acts to protect not only themselves but their child. True to Hollywood convention, Butcher is a terrible man with his longer hair and wilder look offering a typical representation of the cruel assassin, also reflected in the representation of Chris, one of the main assassins in *The*

Wire. The main purpose of Butcher is for us to dislike him more than Tsotsi and therefore to feel no particular remorse when Tsotsi is forced to sacrifice him himself in order to save the father of the child.

In this sequence, the gang has returned to the house, or at least Tsotsi has returned, the gang is not aware of his previous crime. The gang ties up the father (played by Raulana Seiphemo) and raids the fridge and the rooms until the father sets off the alarm with his car keys. Butcher decides to finish the job and Tsotsi shoots him, just in time, in true Hollywood style. This moment also establishes a relationship between the father (character name John) and Tsotsi, which makes the outcome of the film a little more believable. Tsotsi has saved this man's life at great cost to his own. He has sacrificed a friend, a killer himself, but part of his own brotherhood. In that moment we see that Tsotsi is not an easy killer like Butcher, but someone who is beginning to understand the cost of parenthood. Although he has broken into the house to get milk for the child, he has perhaps already committed to returning the baby to its proper life.

The Pipes

Juxtaposition is used to represent the differences between the child that David (Tsotsi) has stolen and his own life. Tsotsi takes the child to a set of pipes where he found shelter as an abandoned child. There, he reflects upon the home he had, or did not have. This contrasts to the wealth of the baby he has stolen. There is no hope for Tsotsi to inherit that lifestyle, or to get back what he has lost, but the juxtaposition of the wealth of the baby with the poverty of the street children and Tsotsi's pipe represents not only Tsotsi's dilemma but that of South Africa and perhaps much of Africa itself. Tsotsi makes his decision and only just in time; his decency is given only minutes to represent itself before Soekie, the barkeeper, reports him.

The Semiotics of Decency

As a representation of his new-found decency he puts on his white shirt, gathers up the baby and takes money to the old beggar as he passes by on his journey to the house. Once at the gate he could leave the baby and run, but he chooses to tell the parents that the baby is there. At this point the ending is very different to the one in the book. The modern retelling deals with the modern South Africa, the concept of a black middle class. The gate divides the rich from the poor; it protects and also makes vulnerable. The gate is an icon of the modern South Africa – quite often it does not work.

What Tsotsi does is the nightmare of every middle class South African when the gate breaks down and he steals the car, the baby and wounds the mother. The gate only works if the individual is safe behind it. In the last scene, the gate acts as bars across the divide, prison bars that Tsotsi cannot cross, until the owner, who calls him 'brother', opens the gate. The colour of their skin is the one thing that cannot divide them. Tsotsi has found decency, but has he now found redemption?

REDEMPTION

The redemption narrative is a standard Hollywood convention. It is a convenient device for the despatching of sympathetic characters who have done terrible things, or who started out as evil and gradually, through the process of the story, redeemed themselves. A famous if somewhat clichéd representation of the redemption narrative is in *The Poseidon Adventure*, (dir. Ronald Neame, 1972) where the drunken priest, long since divest of his faith, cynical and drunk, plunges to the flames cursing his faith but redeeming himself and others by sacrificing himself on behalf of the other passengers.

Needless to say, Stephen King's *Shawshank Redemption* (dir. Frank Darabont, 1994) deals, at the very least, with the redemption narrative associated with Morgan Freeman as he gradually comes to genuinely regret the crimes of his youth. In *Man on Fire* (dir. Tony Scott, 2004) Denzel Washington's character is a former 'wet-boy' (counter insurgency assassin) who has grown weary of the killing he has witnessed and perpetrated. His redemption requires sacrifice in the saving of a little girl and the exposing of men much worse than himself.

A much more sophisticated version of the redemption narrative comes in the film *Road to Perdition* (dir. Sam Mendes, 2002). None of the characters in that film are particularly worthy of redemption. They are gangsters and killers, they commit terrible acts of murder and each one of them must die for it. The main character, played by Tom Hanks, is amongst the worst of them, but what redeems him is his love for his son. He goes to all lengths to protect him, but so awful are the acts that he commits that he too must die. Such a protagonist can no more be allowed to survive than the evil antagonists he faces. It is a powerful and violent film, but in the end cleans up nicely, Hanks' character dies saving his son. The character has literally 'redeemed' his son from death and, by doing so, has redeemed himself as a human being. He too has demonstrated decency, and once again it is parenting and family that exposes this decency.

African Redemption

The Hollywood redemption narrative, even at its most complex, still tends to the neat solution. The narratives in world cinema, independent film and *Tsotsi* are not so neat, even if redemption is a part of the plot.

Redemption, of course, is a useful device as it does allow, if not for a happy ending, then for a positive resolution. Death redeems almost arbitrarily; the death of the violent protagonist redeems his or her humanity and solves the problem of what they might do with the rest of their lives. What, for instance, would the Leonardo di Caprio's character do with the rest of his life at the end of *Blood Diamond* (dir. Edward Zwick, 2007) considering his violent and merciless history?

An earlier film set in 1950's Kenya, *The Kitchen Toto* (dir. Harry Hook, 1987), makes no such use of the positive properties of death and no one in the film, including the innocent, is redeemed or saved. Perhaps for that reason it is one of the least watched, most underrated films, not even on the market now. However, it remains one of the most effective and affecting representations of a childhood in East Africa from both the white and the black point of view, portraying the divisions as bleak, divisive and, most of all, irredeemable.

Tsotsi comes somewhere between the representation of redemption as a complete and neat end to a story, and the bleak and unredeemed ending of *The Kitchen Toto*. There is no easy answer for the protagonist. He commits horrible crimes and seems not to regret them. He is a predator who hunts down the vulnerable and the innocent. But he is not a wild character observed from the outside, as Cuba Gooding Jnr. observes Ice Cube in *Boyz n the Hood* (dir. John Singleton, 1991), or as Colin Farrell is observed in *Tigerland* (dir. Joel Schumacher, 2000) or even *City of God*, (dir. Fernando Meirelles, 2002).

These films tends to depict the worst characters from the point of view of an observer, someone who later becomes a writer, a photographer or at least moves on, and who looks back on these characters with a combination of sympathy and horror. *Tsotsi* allows the audience no such luxury; we are invited to share the life of a protagonist, who, by any standards, would usually be an antagonist. There is no distance from this character, no method by which the audience is set apart, no narrator to soften the blow. He is, as his name suggests, a thief, a thug, a hoody with a gun.

He has more in common with the wrong side of the law crime representations that crowd our television screens, from *Kidulthood* (dir. Menhaj Huda, 2006) to *The Wire*, through *CSI* and *The Bill*, than with the heroic representations of young people making their way in battle or through college or in romantic comedy. The only mitigating factor is his youth. When casting the role it was decided to make the character young, since it was felt the audience would be able to sympathise with a youth making terrible mistakes rather than an older man with too long a history of violence.

Tsotsi must take the audience with him on his journey to decency via some form of redemption. In the tradition of Hollywood redemption, this process does require him to kill someone worse than him, at least to demonstrate that he does have some redeemable features. The killing of Butcher to save the child's father fulfils all the elements of parental redemption. The return of the baby, of course, demonstrates that he has achieved some form of understanding of right and wrong, which again makes him a candidate for redemption.

The recognition of his own responsibility hints at his readiness for redemption. He refuses to let Miriam take the baby, even though it might have been safer for her and it would have allowed him to get away with it. The fact that he recognises his own role in the return of the baby and is willing to risk something of himself to do the right thing makes him redeemable. Even Miriam relents and recognises the evidence of insipient decency. At this stage, one way to redeem him would be to have him sacrifice his own life in the interests of the baby, perhaps to be shot by the angry father as he is trying to return the baby, or to make the standard gesture of going for a gun to allow the police to shoot him in good conscience.

(Spoiler warning – do not read on if you do not want to know what happens in the novel.)

In fact in the book Tsotsi does die in a hopeless attempt to rescue the baby from the destruction of his township home by the bulldozers sent in to clear the unsightly illegal townships. However, the end of the film leaves Tsotsi to face the consequences of his actions, an ending that Hollywood protagonists or antagonists rarely have to face. Only in films such as *American History X* (dir. Tony Kaye, 1999) do the characters have to face the lifelong knowledge of a wrong done that cannot be undone.

The end of *Tsotsi* presents the audience and Tsotsi with just that prospect. There is no escape for him and he must face the consequences of his action. He chooses to do the right thing. This is action and consequence at work. There may be no escape for Tsotsi but there may be hope. He is still alive and the subtle performance of the white policeman, Captain Smit, played by Ian Roberts, hints at some kind of sympathy and the father of the stolen child calls him brother.

In the circle on the road in the final scene, all of South Africa is represented: the doomed and violent street kid with nowhere to go; the volatile, newly-powerful black policeman; the experienced, hard-bitten white policemen who has seen much change and may have much to regret; the young security man working for a global organisation (ADT) that now has permission to trade in South Africa, and the black middle class family.

THE BOOK

Modern Themes

The last scene and the way it differs from the last scene in the book is, perhaps, an indication of the modernised story of *Tsotsi* to take on board the themes and issues that dominate not just South Africa but the whole of South Africa. Throughout the film, the dominant indexical signifiers are the posters that warn against HIV and Aids. They populate the metro and hint at the fundamental issue that blights Africa's progress. Whilst it is not said, it is clear that David's (Tsotsi's) mother is dying of AIDS. She, like so many women in Africa, is a victim of the ignorance of the disease and the culture of multiple. The indexical signifiers on the metro and the vision of the woman in the bed are all we need to understand that this Tsotsi inhabits a modern South Africa with an all too modern scourge.

In this way, the film has updated the book. The script was written using the book as a basis and much of the dialogue and characterisation remains the same. Costumes may differ of course. Tsotsi does not wear a suit and trilby but a black leather jacket and a hoody. The image of the thug is updated. However the film updates other aspects of the book, which is in some ways bleaker.

The Black Middle Class

The film has Tsotsi stealing a Mercedes (the icon of wealth across the world) from a woman as she is trying to enter her house. The gate itself is a modern signifier of South African life. It welcomes the owner yet keeps out the uninvited guest. It should keep the inhabitants secure, but it is a machine and if it fails to recognise its owner then the playing field is levelled and all the money and privilege cannot protect those outside from the same issues as those that face the squatters in the townships.

Tsotsi puts up his hood, steals the car at gunpoint, and shoots the woman when she tries to get into the car. This is a seemingly inexplicable act until we understand that it is not the car she dreads losing but the child. He leaves her wounded, in fact paralysed, like the dog that his father paralyses with a vicious kick, like the disabled beggar who begins to uncover his decency.

The theme of the black middle class is a new representation in itself. It challenges the endless stereotypes of African people as homeless, warring and tribal. These are ordinary people in a nice house, surrounding themselves with the accoutrements of every wealthy family – a nursery, toys, TV and sophisticated living. We do not ever know what they do, but John, the father, wears a suit and they have a Mercedes. They have a lot to lose, a lot to protect.

In the book, the mother of the baby has only her life to lose. After Tsotsi has beaten Boston, he runs across the wasteland and sees a young woman clutching a shoebox. He assumes, rightly, that the box must contain something valuable as she holds it so tightly. He stalks her and then approaches. In the subsequent struggle, she hands him the shoebox in exchange for her life and runs off into the dark. He is left, literally holding the baby.

This is a bleak representation of the toll that poverty takes on a young woman in South Africa. Her back story is never told, perhaps it is loneliness, and perhaps it is rape, youth or just sheer poverty. Tsotsi would have looked wealthy and perhaps we are meant to think that he is better able to feed it. Whatever, Tsotsi is left with no obligation to the mother in the book, only to the baby.

The use of the black middle class in the film does allow a new look at the new South Africa. It speaks to a universal fear that the haves may lose what they have to the have-nots. This is a theme that anyone can relate to, and the audience is not alienated by the idea that a woman might give her child away, for whatever reason.

Townships

Whilst the townships remain an issue in the modern South Africa, they are in the process of being subsumed into urban life. There are still many illegal squatters, many people who are unable to make their own living beyond the barest minimum, but as a scourge AIDS is the modern enemy. In the 1950s the townships were illegal, according to the whites, and they were bulldozed to the ground arbitrarily by the whites. It is against this background that Fugard sets his story. In updating it Hood, as a white South African, has woven in the themes of decency in the face of poverty with the challenges of modern South African history.

Activity

Tsotsi and the beggar

Tsotsi is the kind of man whose attention people do not want, so when the disabled beggar shouts at him for tripping over his paralysed legs, Tsotsi focuses on him as prey. As a pivotal scene in the film, it points forward to Tsotsi's developing sense of decency, but also back to the memories he has buried and must now face to recognise the source of his own indecency.

This sequence is a good one to use as a basis of textual analysis of a scene. The shot includes:

1. close-ups, particularly from a low angle on Tsotsi as he grows more threatening

2. intimate detail – close-ups on the faces of the two reveal the changes in Tsotsi's mood and the intimate, almost painful, agony of the old man

3. power shots – as Tsotsi threatens the old man he is shot from a low angle, but as he begins to relinquish his power and reveal something of himself the camera films the old man from a low angle

4. two shots – there are wide two shots against the background of urban isolation

5. representation of a broken back – the old man is paralysed and this stirs the memory of Tsotsi's dog, crippled by his father's vicious kick. In the book the disabled beggar drags himself on the ground without a wheelchair. Visually, this might have been too much of an obvious link for film, but the paralysis has its parallel nevertheless

6. Tsotsi walks away he follows the railway tracks – isolated
   from the landscape on a linear journey away from it. In the
   book this is the way Tsotsi thinks of his life, as if he were
   moving along a railway (DVD 27: 50).

Activity – use this chart to define the characters of the
standard protagonist and antagonist. Then chart how
Tsotsi represents them both.

Protagonist	Antagonist	*Tsotsi*

Endnotes

49   His act of cutting himself as he challenges Tsotsi is a strong representation of the
      motivation behind self harm.

50   The MacGuffin was a plot device that Hitchcock used to progress the plot. It was the
      secrets in North By North West or the money in Psycho, not really relevant except to the
      journey that the characters take.

51   Athol Fugard Tsotsi, pub. Canongate. P.43.

52   Athol Fugard Tsotsi, pub. Canongate. P7.

53   The Wire Season 4 Episode 11 is a good one.

54   The programme of actions that alcoholics embark upon in order to recover from

      alcoholism and repair damaged relationships.

Bibliography

Aristotle, *Poetics*, Penguin Classics, 2003

Bruno Bettelheim, *The Uses of Enchantment*, Penguin Books, 1991

David Bordwell, *Narration in Film Fiction*, Madison: University of Wisconsin Press 2005

David Bordwell, *Making Meaning: Inference and Rhetoric in the Interpretation of Cinema* Cambridge: Harvard University Press, 1989

Michael Caine, *What's It All About?* pub. Arrow Books. 1993

Peter Davis, *Darkest Hollywood*, Ohio University Press, 1996

E. Annie Proulx. *Brokeback Mountain*, Fourth Estate, 1998

Athol Fugard, *Tsotsi*, Canongate, 2006

John de Graaf, David Wann, Thomas H Naylor, and Vicki Robin, *Aflluenza: The All Consuming Epidemic*, Berrett-Koehler, 2005

Ed. June Givanni & Imruh Bakari, *Symbolic Narratives/ African Cinema: Audiences, Theory and the Moving Image* Bfi Publishing, 2000

Trevor Huddleston, *Naught for Your Comfort*, Collins 1958

Jacqueline Maingard, *South African National Cinema*, Routledge, 2006

Ellen Wilkie with Judith Gunn, *A Pocketful of Dynamite*, Hodder 1990

Donald Woods, *Asking for Trouble*, Penguin Books, 1987

Vladímir Propp, *Morphology Of The Folk Tale* 1928 Translation ©1968, The American Folklore Society and Indiana University

Webography

www.tsotsi.com

www. motion.kodak.com/motion/uploadedFiles/tsotsi.pdf

http://www.country-data.com/cgi-bin/query/r-12090.html

http://www.ukfilmcouncil.org.uk/10300

http://www.independent.co.uk/arts-entertainment/films/
features/how-film-fans-fell-in-love-with-subtitles-462402.
html

http://www.imdb.com/title/tt0709116/

Source http://uk.imdb.com/name/nm0004303/

http://www.youtube.com/watch?v=uV3nFwUlkYM&feature=ch
annel_page

www.anc.org.za/ancdocs/history/misc/verkuyl.html

http://www.davidbordwell.net/books/index.php#meaning

http://mural.uv.es/vifresal/Propp.htm

http://www.mythfolklore.net/3043mythfolklore/reading/remus/
extras/1881_introduction.htm

http://www.bbc.co.uk/eastenders/characters_cast/characters/
character_rickyb.shtml

http://www.corrie.net/profiles/characters/barlow_ken.html

http://adage.com/century/icon01.html

http://www.guardian.co.uk/film/2007/sep/28/1

http://www.hbo.com/thewire/

http://www.christiantoday.com/article/methodist.spirituality.
meetings.planned.amid.shocking.youth.statistics/3829.htm

http://www.courttv.com/archive/legaldocs/misc/killers.html

http://www.nndb.com/people/666/000023597/

http://www.trutv.com/library/crime/notorious_murders/
celebrity/natural_born_killers/1.html

http://www.thedailyshow.com/video/index.jhtml?videoId=18847
3&title=10,000-McCainiacst

http://www.aber.ac.uk/media/Documents/short/trans.html

http://business.pearlanddean.com/marketdata/audience.html

Studying
The Devil's Backbone
James Rose

Also available in this series

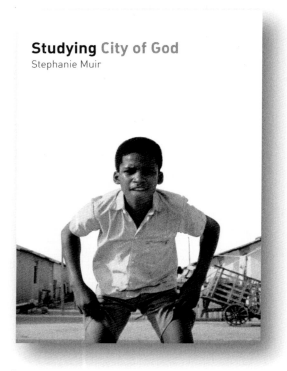

Studying City of God
Stephanie Muir

> "This is one of the best study guides I have seen... you would be foolish indeed to ignore this guide. "
>
> *In the Picture*